POETRY REVIEW

SPRING 2001 VOLUME
EDITOR PETER FOR
PRODUCTION JANET PH
ADVERTISING LISA RO

CW01472191

CONTENTS

Seven Years On: A New Generation Retrospective

National Poetry Competition

Appreciations

All illustrations by Gerald Mangan

Seven Years On – Part 2

The Summer *Poetry Review* continues our survey into the state of play in poetry seven years after New Generation Poets.

Poets featured include: Patience Agbabi, Charles Boyle, Alison Brackenbury, Colette Bryce, Harry Clifton, James Fenton, John Fuller, Mark Halliday, Brian Henry, John Kinsella, James Lasdun, Edwin Morgan, Craig Raine, Maurice Riordan, Carole Satyamurti, John Stammers, Greta Stoddart, George Szirtes, Sarah Wardle, Susan Wicks, and many more

Plus: An Interview with Edwin Morgan
         The Dearmer Prize Shortlist

Published July 15

P O E T R Y   R E V I E W

POETRY REVIEW
SUBSCRIPTIONS
Four issues including postage:

UK individuals £27
Overseas individuals £35
(all overseas delivery is by airmail)
USA individuals $56

Libraries, schools and institutions:
UK £35
Overseas £42
USA $66

Single issue £6.95 + 50p p&p (UK)

Sterling and US dollar payments only. Eurocheques, Visa and Mastercard payments are acceptable.

Bookshop distribution:
Signature
Telephone 0161 834 8767

Design by Philip Lewis
Cover by Janet Phillips
Cover image © PhotoDisc, Inc

Typeset by Poetry Review.

Printed by Newnorth Print Ltd at Newnorth House, College Street Kempston, Bedford MK42 8NA
Telephone: 01234 341111

POETRY REVIEW is the magazine of the Poetry Society. It is published quarterly and issued free to members of the Poetry Society. Poetry Review considers submissions from non-members and members alike. To ensure reply submissions must be accompanied by an SAE or adequate International Reply coupons: Poetry Review accepts no responsibility for contributions that are not reply paid.

Founded 24 February 1909
Charity Commissioners No: 303334
© 2001

Funded by
THE ARTS COUNCIL
OF ENGLAND

EDITORIAL AND BUSINESS ADDRESS:
22 BETTERTON STREET, LONDON WC2H 9BX

telephone   020 7420 9880   fax 020 7240 4818
email   poetryreview@poetrysoc.com ISBN 1 900 771 24 1
website   http://www.poetrysoc.com   ISSN 0032 2156

The Poetry Society is supported by
BT

SEVEN YEARS ON

by Peter Forbes

AT THE TIME of the New Generation Poets promotion in 1994 it was objected a) that this was no generation (in the sense that the poets should all know each other and be mutually influenced) and b) that they weren't new. Seven years on anyone taking the pulse of contemporary poetry, which this and the next issue of *Poetry Review* intend to do, has to recognize that there *is* a dominant group of poets in the country who *are* influenced by each other, many of whom *were* chosen for New Generation. Several members of this current group were not in New Generation, however, mostly because of the forty-year-old cut-off point, but would not deny their close connections today. The original list of New Generation Poets is now history; we can concentrate on who are the most productive and creative poets today.

The members of this group of mainstream-poets-who-are-currently-making-the-running (they need a handy name but we'll come to that later) have been winning the prizes in the last few years: Carol Ann Duffy (virtually everything); Sean O'Brien (Forward), Don Paterson (Eliot and Forward First), Michael Donaghy (Forward), John Burnside (Whitbread), Jamie McKendrick (Forward), Jo Shapcott (Forward), Ruth Padel (National Poetry Competition), Ian Duhig (National Poetry Competition), Paul Farley (Forward First Collection). Prizes may not sell many extra copies of books but they play an important role in the consolidation of poetic reputations.

Identifying and creating "movements" has been a part of the poetry game since time dot; this time it is easier to recognize the group than to characterize it. Twenty years ago Peter Porter (see p. 61) presciently identified the first stirrings of this movement; as he says, he wasn't sure what to call them – "Provincial Dandies" or "North of England Surrealists" – but he always knew who they were. At the time, the writers concerned were all male: O'Brien, Didsbury, Houston with, a few years later, Paterson, Duhig etc. Now that the generation is in full flood with (as Don Paterson points out in his piece on p. 4) a decent complement of women, it is possible to be a bit more precise. "Shape-shifters", the term used by Jo Shapcott in her interview (p. 18) might be appropriate. What the poets have in common is a penchant for transformation over literal scene-setting. (Many of the poets contributed to *After Ovid* a few years ago, and Ovid is the ur-Shape-shifter. This can make their poetry seem difficult, hence Don Paterson's new slogan: *Read Poetry: It's Really Quite Hard.*

Don Paterson and many others in the poetry world believe that there is an inherent contradiction between this difficulty and the concerted efforts made since New Generation to market poetry as an accessible art in a dumbed-down age. But Carol Ann Duffy and Simon Armitage are serious, uncompromising artists who have become popular, so there must be some hope that the strongest voices will find readers.

For this issue we have focussed on a range of poets far wider than any recognisable group: from Seamus Heaney to Elizabeth Bartlett. At any time in poetry, the best poetry being written will sometimes come from representative figures but just as often it will come from lone mavericks. To corral both types in one issue is more appealing – to this editor, at least – than playing a rigid game of inclusion and exclusion. One of the fascinations of soliciting work from so many poets is that a kind of snapshot is produced. The work that comes in might tell you more about the Zeitgeist and who's influencing whom than any amount of theorizing on the subject.

The prevalence of scientific themes in the work that came in was striking, so striking that these poems have been grouped together. There are other similarities: much of the poetry being written now has an excited, celebratory character, even if, as in Sean O'Brien's poetry, the subject matter is often inherently downbeat. These poets are excited by the possibilities of language. The world is often seen as a riot of sensation; there is a playful fantastical feel to much of it. Sometimes it is science that provides the hyper-real element, sometimes it is sex. One could argue that many poets today have thrown off the rather dour, cautious English empiricist mode in favour of a more Latin, carnivalesque way of seeing the world. Given the current doubts that afflict the English re: the loss of a sense of identity, the confidence of the poets has to be a cause for celebration.

The Legacy of NewGen

by Don Paterson

SHORTLY AFTER THE New Generation promotion hit the beach, I received a phonecall from Michael Donaghy.

"Hey Don – I've had this guy on the phone looking for you".

"Oh really?"

"Yeah. He got my number from the Poetry Society and then asked if I could put you on... he just assumed we were all living in one big house. Y'know. Like the Monkees."

***

While it would be churlish to deny that the NewGen publicity helped some of us a whole lot, many of us also spent years getting it in the neck for something that didn't actually happen. NewGen consisted of a few photocalls, an appearance on TV and two or three gigs. That was it. For whatever reason, though, the stakes are now perceived to be worth fighting for in a way they weren't before NewGen. (They aren't, never have been, and by and large are as low as ever. Blessedly – despite everyone's best and worst efforts – poetry continues to be its own reward; this will continue to guarantee its amateur status among the arts. Though you would never think so, given the number of younger poets that now talk of their "career". *Writing poetry? A career?*) This has afforded the jealous and the thwarted a far clearer sense of *project* than their jealousy and thwartedness entitled them to ten years ago.

***

NewGen was one of the more visible manifestations of a general trend – a trend which mired us deeper in a lot of bad things: the cult of the individual voice, the cult of youth, the silly dogma of "show not tell" (fine advice for beginners, but an insane line for an experienced practitioner to tow), and worst of all, the provincialism of the contemporary. I recently sat in a room listening to a certain eminent *litterateuse* enquire of the air why anyone, in 2001, for God's sake, would want to write like Louis MacNeice. Well, y'know. If you have to ask.

***

But it *was* a good generation. Not great, maybe, but certainly good. The generation above produced a handful of poets who attained heights that very few in ours will equal, if any do at all. (A handful of others seem to have already secured for themselves that most gently damning of epitaphs: *he was a poet praised mainly by novelists*.) And ours also had, for the first time, a decent number of women; not the correct number, but a decent one.

The generation below us... ach. Sorry to say this, but I see no Maxwell, no Burnside, no Jamie, no Donaghy, no Duffy, no Hofmann... I could go on, and for quite a bit. (And that's without invoking the O'Briens and Shapcotts and Didsburys who were excluded from the promotion by NewGen's ageist selection criteria.) There are five or six serious talents, and a lot of terrifyingly competent versifiers; professional, even. Professionalism is what happens when ambition drifts away from the poem and towards the poet. So it sometimes seems as if NewGen condemned at least part of the next Gen to self-consciousness (either through imitation, or the deliberate avoidance of it) and careerism. A few among them – Alice Oswald springs to mind – have made a point of removing themselves completely from the scene, partly to avoid contamination by its real or perceived values. I don't blame them.

***

After NewGen, reviewing got much worse. I've been back and had a look. It was always terrible, but far too many reviews now seem to fall into one of two categories: elegant vituperation and semiliterate praise. Writers such as John Kinsella – as eloquent in their advocacy as their criticism, and alive to the whole spectrum of the art – are depressingly thin on the ground.

(The kind of review that shits from a great height on a book is almost invariably – you have to make exceptions – written out of a snivelling insecurity, regardless of its apparent swagger. It shouldn't be read as anything but a snapshot of the author's psychopathology. I know, because I wrote a ton of them. Artificially pumped full of the confidence I thought I was supposed to feel – but somehow didn't – as a NewGen poet, I came on like a young gunslinger, and wrote reviews that were pointlessly cruel, and disgracefully *ad hominem*. I only quit when one review provoked a well-orchestrated series of death-threats from friends of my victim. You have to realise when you're crap at something.)

***

Advice read too late (Cioran, somewhere): if you want to neutralise your enemies, *speak well of them everywhere*.

***

Forgive me for banging on about this, but it's important: reviewing, while it was not an exercise I managed to perform with any grace, should be a pretty straightforward business. It's a matter of divining the ambition of the work (its degree, as well as direction) and then fairly assessing its shortfall. You do this by holding it up to the accepted gold standards of the genre. You don't judge a poem of Sophie Hannah's by how far short you might feel it to fall of 'Briggflatts' or 'A Disused Shed'. You might look instead at Swift or De La Mare or Housman or Betjeman or Cope.

There recently appeared in these pages a review, by Rod Mengham, of Billy Collins' last book. As Billy's editor, I know that he doesn't need me to defend him; I raise the matter to illustrate a point. Collins is a humane, wise, funny and gentle poet that Mr Mengham dismissed as an idiot, on the grounds – as far as I could infer – that he wasn't Lyn Hejinian. All this smacked of a man paying to watch a football game, and then demanding a refund at halftime because it wasn't a cricket match. You can only compare like with like. And if you don't have a "like" to adduce – one that you yourself can defend and champion – you are, by definition, rather ill-qualified to discuss the matter. An act of criticism which has as its implicit premise the rejection of an entire genre is a) perfectly worthless, and b) a form of higher illiteracy. And – though I personally enjoy Collins' work a great deal – I believe that it's important to argue for, and even enthusiastically promote, work you admire but don't necessarily *like*. And if, for you, the two are exactly the same thing... you are either God-like in the immaculacy of your good taste, or in the grip of a terrific self-delusion.

Okay; all this seems rather a lot to blame on NewGen, but the creation of its charmed circle split the camps, and widened the divisions between those that were split already. The brashness of the

campaign meant that this happened in a pretty irreparable way, when it might have brought the sides closer together. It made sensible dialogue between them all the harder, and their terminal irreconcilability now allows – see above – mere prejudice to masquerade as considered opinion. (And rereading that last para, I can see I'm just as disinclined to do *my* bit to effect the *rapprochement*.) Which quite accidentally brings me to my next point.

***

I quite agree that the NewGen were a bit too homogenous a group. Iain Sinclair dismissed the lot of us as "pod people", and I concede at least half the point. The poets he collected in his *Conductors of Chaos* were just from another pod – however infinitely various they may feel themselves to be – but some deserved, and have never received, proper attention. Exactly the same goes for performance poets. A whole lot of useful cross-pollination could have taken place that didn't. Denise Riley and Jean Breeze on the same stand; why the hell not? In retrospect, I think Carol Ann Duffy was quite right to exempt herself from the promotion; none of the rest of us did, simply because we couldn't afford to.

***

The best thing to come out of NewGen was the chance for poets at opposite ends of the country to meet up and talk to each other; the friendships made resulted in several of us having a profound influence on one another's work. All this makes it a crying shame that there weren't far more poets involved. NewGen also kickstarted a much more professional approach to the marketing of poetry, which it badly needed. (But that's *poetry*, as opposed to some twenty-year old advertising copywriter's idea of what poetry might be. Take, for example, the idiocy of last year's National Poetry Day "Fresh Voices" promotion, when we were invited to suggest a poem that might serve as a natalitial for Leo Blair, Rocco Ciccone and Brooklyn Beckham.)

A lot of the outreach work seems to have forgotten poetry's natural constituency. By that I mean the literate classes – many of them, unfashionably and through no fault of their own, middle. There's no reason why the theatre-going, serious-novel-buying public shouldn't be reading poetry too. Not nearly enough of them are. Now before someone willfully misinterprets this as an attack on the invaluable work that has been done in schools, prisons, M&S, youth clubs and council chambers – my point is simply that the war has to be waged on all fronts, and the front that would have fallen most easily has been among the most neglected.

The constant dumbing down of poetry promotion makes this a more distant goal than ever, though. A message can be simplified to the point where it says precisely the opposite of what it originally intended. I'm all in favour of the old consciousness-raising exercise; but consciousness of *what*? At the moment National Poetry Day is doing for poetry what Paddy's Day is doing for the Irish problem. NewGen may have sinned gravely in its omissions, and focused on poets, not poems – but at least it was conceived with some integrity and very little cynicism. Were the same people to do it again, it would doubtless be done differently, and better. It was a naive time for all of us.

***

Kingsley Amis once dreamt up a brilliant advertising campaign for alcohol, along the lines of: *Drink Beer. It Makes You Drunk*. It works, because the selling point also happens to be an intrinsic property of the thing you're advertising. If you have to go looking for it – *Beer Makes You Look Sexy,*

Beer Brings You Closer to God – you should really be selling something different, like lingerie or religion. Anyway here's my slogan: *Read Poetry. It's Really Quite Hard*. This will appeal immediately to the target audience (aye, the literate classes; why does that always sound like a heresy?) who will be thoroughly intrigued, and then – as we all know – deeply rewarded for the investment poetry will ask of them. It also has the merit of throwing the emphasis back on the poem, where perhaps it should have been in the first place.

***

National Poetry Day. I forget the year. I receive a call – in my capacity as NewGen poet, I assume, since the caller thinks I am Michael Donaghy – asking me to appear on *Newsnight*. The researcher suggests that I might want to talk about how poetry has been trivialised by the media. I laboriously put my case. "Yeah!" she exclaims. "Just the sort of thing we're looking for. Now – if we send a cab over at half past five, do you think you might put these thoughts into verse?" I looked at my watch: it was half-past four. I will spare you my response.

DON PATERSON

In competition terms, Don Paterson has probably been the most successful of the New Generation poets after Carol Ann Duffy. He has won most of the prizes: the Arvon for 'A Private Bottling' (1994), the Forward First Collection for *Nil, Nil* (Faber, 1993) and the T. S. Eliot for *God's Gift to Women* (Faber, 1997). *God's Gift to Women* marked Paterson's ascendancy to a position alongside Simon Armitage as the most admired poets of their born-1962-3 generation. It features more of the postmodernist extravaganza 'The Alexandrian Library', some lugubrious *noirish* violence ("I killed the alarm, // then took her head off with the kitchen knife / with no more malice than I might a rose / for my daily buttonhole...") and also has moments of great lyrical beauty. The conflict between Paterson's MacNeicean lyric streak and the post-modernist demands of the age is not yet resolved. His acclaimed versions of Machado's poems in *The Eyes* (Faber, 1999) neatly side-step the problem by using someone else's poems that are unashamedly lyrical.

THE FOREST OF THE SUICIDES
Inferno, canto xiii

Nessus was still midriver, trotting back
to the far bank, when suddenly I found
myself in a dark wood, this time unmarked
by any path at all. I looked around.

Each barren, blood-black tree was like a plate
from a sailor's book of knots, its branches bent
and pleached and coiled as if to demonstrate
some novel or ingenious brand of torment.

In the topmost branches of those wretched trees
I saw the Snatcher build its nest, whose kin
drove Aeneas from the Strophades,
spoiled his table, and spat out his ruin.

There it squats, its human face all wrong
above its fledged gut, wide-winged, razor-clawed.
With its avian knack of mimicry, its song
is a loop-tape of the children it has tortured.

I felt so desolate, it gave me a start
to hear his voice. "Now friend, before we leave
stand still for just a moment, and listen hard.
What you'll hear is almost too strange to believe".

Below the pitiful sobs and chokes and cries
lower moans were echoing through the glade,
and yet I saw no one to make them. "Master, why
do they hide from us?" I asked. "Are they afraid?"

Then he replied: "Break off a little spray
from any of those plants: I guarantee
things will become clearer." I snapped away
a twig from the bush that stood closest to me.

In the trunk a red mouth opened like a cut.
Then a voice screamed out "Why are you tearing me?"
It was a woman's voice. Blood began to spurt
from the broken tip. "You, are you hearing me?

When exactly did I earn *your* scorn?
Supposing I'd a heart black as a snake's,
I was a woman once, that now am thorn –
what would a little pity have set you back?"

Just in the way a split cord of green wood,
lit at one end, starts to spit and blister
at the other, so it was the words and blood
bubbled from her splintered mouth. "Dear sister",

my guide interrupted, "if only my poor friend
had recalled what I had written of this hell
I know he never would have raised his hand
against you; but the truth is so incredible

I urged him on. Forgive his ignorance –
but he can make amends; just tell him who
you were, and how you came here. When he returns
to the upper world, your fame can bloom anew".

But the tree laughed. "Bravo sir! Well said.
You'd spend a lifetime trying to put it worse.
In my design, that scalded beach ahead
would be reserved for the biographers.

And if it's self-improvement your friend seeks
perhaps it's courtesy you need to teach . . .
Ah. But you can see that I am weak,
and lured into a little human speech.

Very well. When I was small, I held both keys
that fitted my father's heart – which I unlocked
and locked again with such a delicate ease
he felt no turning, and he heard no click.

He desired no other confidence but mine;
nor would I permit one. I was so bound
to my splendid office that, when he resigned,
I followed. They had to dig me from the ground.

So the post remained, and I remained as true;
and, in time, I came to interview
for his successor. None of them would do
until a black shape cut the light in two

and at once I knew my ideal candidate.
But that green-eyed courtesan, that vice of courts
who had always stalked his halls and watched his gate –
the years had steeped me in her sullen arts

and my tongue grew hot with her abysmal need.
Slowly, I turned it on my second Caesar
until it seemed to him his every deed
did nothing but disgrace his predecessor.

So he left me too; but the tongue still burned away
till I sung the bright world only to estrange it,
and prophesied my end so nakedly
mere decency insisted I arrange it.

My mind, then, in its voice of reasoned harm
told me Death would broker my release
from every shame, and back into his arms;
so I made my date. It was bad advice.

But if your friend should somehow cut a path
back to the world, tell them this: that I betrayed
the spirit, not the letter of the oath –
by far the lesser crime in our dark trade."

My master hissed: "Listen – she's silent now.
Quickly, don't just throw away your chance;
ask her, if there's more you wish to know."
I replied: "My lord, you know the questions

I bring with me; so ask what I would ask.
I have no stomach for this conversation."
He nodded. "That this man may fulfil his task
and witness for you at his final station,

imprisoned soul – if you could bear to – say
just how the spirit comes to be so caught
in these terrible spasms, and if perhaps one day
it might be wrested free of its own knots."

Minutes passed before she spoke again.
"Remember: though these words are some relief,
the breath I draw to fill them gives a pain
beyond your knowledge. I will be brief.

The very instant that the furious soul
tears itself from the flesh, some inverse power
bundles it screaming down the sudden hole
that opens in the bed or bath or floor;

then Minos directs it to the seventh pit
where it spins down to this starless nursery
to seed wherever fortune tosses it;
there it roots, and drives up through the clay

to grow into the shape of its own anguish.
Finally, the Harpies swarm to crop
the leaves and buds – a blessing and a scourge,
since it pains us, and yet lets the pain escape.

And like you, at the final clarion
we'll return to fish our bodies from the ground,
but never again to wear them: such is the sin
of our ingratitude. Instead, we'll drag them down

to this dark street; and here they'll stay, strung out
forever in their miserable parade –
naked and still, each hung like a white coat
on the hook of its own alienated shade."

GLYN MAXWELL

In 1994 Maxwell was one of the most characteristic figures in New Generation but many found his poems wilfully obscure. His poetry has gradually become more lucid, however, and in *Rest for the Wicked* (Bloodaxe, 1995), his third book, the syntactically-led surrealism had largely disappeared – a poem like 'The Great Detectives' could almost be Auden himself. In 1998 *The Breakage* showed a new departure. The Frostian element is all pervasive: so much so that the sequence 'Letters to Edward Thomas' sometimes sounds authentically Georgian in tone. This book suggests that there is no going back and that the Welwyn brat phase is over. He now lives much of the time in America where he teaches at Amherst College and has started to produce poems reflecting his American ambience. A verse novel, *Time's Fool*, is due from Picador in April.

BLINDFOLD

Far down below, what is in all but truth
the sea lights on Chicago in the dawn.
Waves whiten. Utter distance holds the breath
as if by any ocean. Boats down there
      look tiny, lone
        and fierce as the first stars.

Yet it's a lake, a pool, a pond, it lacks
the open end of *sea* or the way *ocean*
swallows *sea* and pityingly makes
an almost noiseless *n* attempt the sound
      of our perception
        ending. Turn your back.

Blindfold a boy, a lady, set them there:
divest their eyes and watch them see the sea,
the fools, observe them smell salt on the air,
the fools, they might be musing on an iceberg,
      race memory
        afresh on that horizon,

but we who only visit it know more,
and knowledge won't take nothing for a view.
We castellate the line, we feel land there,
cold fishing-ports and cousins we could phone,
      drive to, fly to;
        we talk it to a loop,

and the dreaded sky to airways. Yet we find
at points all morning, at the earthly hours,
the disabused, those of a former mind:
salt at the nostril, mortified by heights
     of fang-black towers –
     they're beggared by the speed

at which after a cent or passing word
their loneliness smacks back in shape like rubber.
Contrariwise went things. The centigrade
will winnow these with skill, as will our hands
     that sort the copper
     faces for what's worth it,

until who comes who's not in on the secret,
in whose eye there is nothing but whose eye,
one whom the light was for, got into, favoured,
who knows no bounds and nothing else, who drops
     from the white sky
     rope ladders that start shaking.

FARM ANIMALS ARE CHILDHOOD

Farm animals are childhood. As we bike past
Massachusetts cows we can't imagine
anything but English – England's version –
smouldering in a cow-brain like compost.

Bikes are childhood. We forked out for these
to ride along this dotted path. The roads
aren't childhood here, so anyone who rides
must overhaul whole biking dynasties.

On a deserted stretch one afternoon
the sun shone and we braked where two small boys
and a big girl were stooping in the trees
beside a fence. The cows stood further on,

vaguely following things with Dorset eyes.
Watching children isn't childhood. Stones
we watched hit the cow flanks, and the cow minds
pieced it together, reckoning otherwise,

as the missed stones fell still and were believed.
Believing's childhood. Caring isn't quite,
and we did more than quite though we did squat,
cared about it, fretted over calves,

phoned the police, the calf-police, some hour
later. They're not childhood on the phone.
Childhood is a well a mile from home,
in which things go on falling till they're here.

Glyn Maxwell's Decade

by Justin Quinn

THOUGH HE WROTE four books totalling four hundred and sixteen pages in the 1990s, Glyn Maxwell would still have difficulty putting together a worthwhile selected poems of over fifty pages; and most of those would be from his first two books, *Tale of the Mayor's Son* (1990) and *Out of the Rain* (1992), while only three each from his last two books, *Rest for the Wicked* (1995) and *The Breakage* (1998), seem to me salvageable*. Despite this slight *oeuvre* and despite the decreasing output of good poems, it seems fair to say that not only was Maxwell one of the most important poets in Britain in the last decade but that he will continue to occupy a central position in the years to come.

It should be immediately conceded that reading his collections through is a numbing experience. So much of what he has published is little more than jam sessions from Welwyn Garden City and Amherst, with all the longueurs and sorting out of leads that jam sessions involve. All is distinctively Maxwellian – the syntax, the speed, the indented stanzas, and above all the tone – but he hits the groove so seldom that he runs the risk of dulling the reader's senses so much that he or she won't recognise the real thing when it arrives. But then, why should a career like Larkin's – little more than a chapbook every decade – be exemplary? The fast-talking sprawl of Maxwell's collections, even if they yielded few good poems, seemed to catch something of the time also. It's unlikely that posterity will be quite so indulgent, but with editorial

discrimination he will be able to winnow poems that will convince all but the most entrenched detractors of his importance.

The title of his first collection set the key note for much of the poetry to come. Not so much a narrative of a set of characters in an English town, but the narrative of those characters as though mediated through a soap-opera. It is clear that Maxwell does not ask for any emotional involvement in their plight – the point lies elsewhere:

The Mayor's son had options. One was death,
   and one was a black and stylish trilby hat
he wore instead, when thinking this: I Love.

The town was not elaborate. The sky
   was white collisions of no special interest
but look at the Mayor's son, at the bazaar!

"I've seen her once before..." Her name was this:
   Elizabeth. The Mayor's son was eighteen,
his mind older than that but his mouth not.

And had no options. "Hey, Elizabeth!"
   I could say what was sold in the bazaar,
I could be clearer on the time of day,

I could define Elizabeth. I will:
   Every girl you ever wanted, but
can't have 'cause I want. She was twenty-one.

Maxwell excels at harnessing Home Counties English in his blank verse. The voice is brash, domineering, and certainly patronising towards the characters. For anyone familiar with the accent and context a line like "I could define Elizabeth. I will", with the last word aggressively emphasised, catches perfectly the bolshy voice of the young English male. The speaker is trying to humiliate the reader. The talk is that of teenage boys with a constant undertow of violence. Later the speaker shouts at the Mayor's son when on the ice rink: "Skate, skate, you're crap at it, // whatever your name is, you Mayor's son". This is a narrator who wants to beat the living daylights out of his characters.

If that was all there were to it, then the poem wouldn't be much more interesting than *Grange Hill*. But Maxwell makes this belligerent speaker the grand panjandrum of the scene and doesn't scruple to let the reader know that he will only reveal so much as serves his own ends. Towns are not usually described as either elaborate or not elaborate – the adjective is more suited to fictions, the quality of the detailing in the background canvas. The speaker is deliberately taunting the reader again with the constructed nature of the scene, as if to say, "Are you such a git to believe *this?*" Of course one doesn't, but what holds the fascination is rather the speed and skill of the speaker himself, for all his obnoxious qualities. Introducing a later scene, the speaker says: "Divide the town into eleven parts, / throw ten of them away, and look at this [...]". And look you will, not because the scene is all that interesting in itself but because of the flourish of the imperatives. The voice is instinct with the snide brashness of those who made it under Thatcherism; also, the figure of dividing up a town and disposing of most of it expertly catches the mood generated in Britain by a state power that acted upon its citizens without scruple.

The volta of the poem comes in the last three stanzas and reveals something far beyond the voice of the postmodernist yob described above:

>   the Mayor
> will be deposed next year: his son will choose
> a university, *it* will say no
>
> to him but take Elizabeth, for Maths
>   not Archaeology, and Alison
> will suddenly, one day, in a Maths class,
>
> befriend Elizabeth, and find that their

acquaintances are mutual, like me
and the Mayor's son, and in a stand-up bar

all evening they'll be there. Meanwhile the books
  will pile up in my world, and someone's hat
will find its way to me and I will wear it.

As events move beyond the enclosure of the town and the teenage world of the actors, reality comes seeping in, and the speaker is no longer a panjandrum of the scene: he does not engineer the trajectory of the hat and his statement that he "will wear it" is less an assertion of will, but of his passive acceptance of a future state of affairs. This is all the more surprising and touching because of the rodomontade that preceded it. For some readers, however, Maxwell does not move beyond the loutish. Perhaps the most sustained and incisive criticism of his work came from Caitriona O'Reilly in *Thumbscrew*. Of 'Tale of the Mayor's Son' she says: "The endless self-interruption, subversive asides and direct addresses to the reader could well be viewed as pyrotechnical cleverness. They are certainly insulting and not very subtle attempts to manipulate the reader". I would respond that the "insulting" aspect of the poem is integral to its success. It is too easy to take offence at Maxwell and not register the degree to which he is thematising the presence of such verbal violence. Of course, the argument of thematisation can seem something of a cop-out, as for instance when Christopher Ricks thus defends T. S. Eliot against anti-Semitism. But the volta of the poem as I have described it confirms that the horizon of the poem is more expansive that O'Reilly would have it.

O'Reilly continues by targeting the poetic self in Maxwell's poetry:

> In his critical study *New Relations* David Kennedy has remarked that "Maxwell's work seems to exist in a species of eternal present, the only available past being that of the author's lifetime". But it is precisely the absence of a believable personal history in Maxwell's work that is so striking. This is partly a result of his postmodern gameplaying, but more straightforwardly reflects a writer with neither a real sense of craft, nor a recognition of the commitment it demands.

It is not clear to me what connection there is between a "believable personal history" and "a real sense of craft" – this would presume that the Confessionals were the only true poetic craftsmen, which I doubt O'Reilly would wish to claim. Does one get such a history from George Herbert, one of the poets she adduces as exemplary in this respect? Certainly, it is a diary of the spirit, but not what would commonly be understood by "believable personal history".

Were he just a post-modern yob Maxwell could never have produced poems like 'I.M. David Penhaligon' and 'Poisonfield' in the same collection, where he displays a convincing civic sense. I quote from the first:

His very name a small peninsula
where people greet and pass the time of day
as if it was their time, not London's time,

he would stand and disarm
the regiment of furious old Coles;
the pleasers and the up-and-coming men

he irritated with a victim's question.

The earnestness and credibility of this voice is the true background for the guffawing in 'Tale of the Mayor's Son'. As political elegy in a book by a twenty-eight-year old this is outstanding. In places it runs the risk of sentimentalising its subject, but this tendency is firmly restrained in the wonderful concluding gesture where Maxwell turns the attention of the poem on the collective, which includes himself. The earnestness of voice in this poem is not often picked up on in responses to his work, and this is unfortunate as it restricts our awareness of his range – and I do not mean here his ability to provide panoramas of contemporary England, rather his emotional register. It is this strand which reappears later in *Rest for the Wicked* (1995) in 'The Sarajevo Zoo', one of the very few successful atrocity-poems of recent times. For the most part this type of poem has the poet wringing his or her hands in front of horrific images on the television. Maxwell uses his characteristic style to intercut between a wide range of images of the war zone, as well as those of home (i.e., safety, where the news is received), forestalling the customary moral platitudes; instead he ushers in a fresh sense of the horror of the situation, as well as the paradox of the deep sympathy felt by viewers and their simultaneous refusal to become involved. He is able to marshal the undertow of violence which was present in 'Tale of the Mayor's Son' to depict a war situation. That his poem partakes of the channel-surfing voyeurism

that most of us will recognise as our own is its strength not its failing, just as his ability to marshal the arrogant voice of Thatcherism in 'Tale' made the poem's turn all the more convincing.

In 'The Altered Slightly' he merges the context of Sarajevo with germ warfare. Such a manoeuvre could so easily collapse into opportunistic conceit (in both senses of the word), but what results instead is an imaginative *jouissance* that fully acknowledges the awfulness of its subject matter:

Hilarious to the virus that has spent
its infinite resources
concocting itself anew,

these healers, helicoptered into a war zone,
with helmets and a peace plan,
pound the maps in a shell of an HQ.

Under the microscope the enemies goggle
in yellow and red grease,
their tricorn shapes a shock, and somebody says

*That's them but if you look
they've altered slightly.* Good news for the sniper
who sights the Muslim wandering up the road,

then sights the Christian limping in the gutter
and cannot choose between them or to let them
come and have each other. The dead,

uniquely in the dark about who did it,
lie still as stone, mistaken for the hiding,
while somewhere in some dedicated rich

lab the virgin germs,
nervous in molecular pitch dark,
parachute into a slide of blood

and set to work.

The poem erases the distinction between tenor and vehicle: microscope and germs are not the means for saying something about the war in the former Yugoslavia, and vice versa. The system of resemblances and echoes is more intricate: the attackers in the germ warfare which ends the poem come out of the dark in which the dead lie; also, their parachuting into the blood is like that of the peacekeepers and antibodies of the first verses. The poem is about the difficulty of recognition, and attendant on this the impossibility of making a moral choice. When one thing flows into the other with such ease, how can one take up a consistent ethical position? These are media-age metamorphoses to equal Ovid, a version of whom follows immediately in the collection. Because Maxwell does not take the trouble to work out the terms of his argument with any precision, he has succeeded in writing a poem which deftly captures the confusions and misrecognitions that are part of our response to modern warfare. He is not sure which side to take, but he is sure about the active presence of destructive agents in the world ("and set to work"). Whether that work is the Devil's or not can't be answered, and a poet who tries relegates him or herself to the lower divisions.

In this context, Maxwell's most recent collection, *The Breakage*, represents a failure of nerve. After the daring of the first books, this collection amounts to little more than a group of obedient exercises in homage to Edward Thomas and Robert Frost. It seems that the transition to middle-age experience and the move to America has presented large problems. Access to the flows of British speech and the sense of thematic complicity with the Sunday supplements is now denied, and he would have no business trying to do the same for America. He is left for the most part with anecdotes about jogging around Amherst, and clearly that does not do it for him as ice-skating in Welwyn did. Nevertheless, there are signs in the book that Maxwell will find ways to think about Britain and his relationship to it even across the oceanic divide. The long sequence 'Letters to Edward Thomas' is an attempt to do this, but apart from the twelfth poem is of little worth. More engaging is 'My Grandfather at the Pool', subtitled 'i.m. James Maxwell 1895–1980' in which he returns to the subject of 'War Hero' from *Out of the Rain*. The speaker of the poem is looking at a photograph of his grandfather with four other young men who are about to dive into a pool. The four are all looking at the camera, Maxwell's grandfather is looking away; the four will die in the trenches, Maxwell's grandfather will survive:

Wholly and coldly gone, they meet our eyes
Like the stars the eye is told are there and tries

To see – all pity flashes back from there,
Till I too am unnamed unaware

And things are stacked ahead of me so vast

I sun myself in shadows that they cast:

Things I dreamed but never dreamed were there,
But are and may by now be everywhere,

When you're what turns the page or looks away.
When I'm what disappears into my day.

This is a dense and demanding conclusion to what has become a set-piece of most collections – photographic ekphrasis. Looking at the photograph, Maxwell sees before him the huge amount of counter-worlds generated by the question "what if it had been otherwise?" Corollary to this is the debt felt towards the fallen, just what Geoffrey Hill says England has ungratefully forgotten. Maxwell's life, in different ways, is beholden to all five men. Whereas Hill tends towards censure, Maxwell is more interested in showing how such issues tilt on a knife-edge in society's recollection. The poem's last line is evocative, implying as it does a bringing together of citizens in honour of the past; as such, Maxwell's poem is not the "deplorable kind of *bien-séance*" that Hill sees in contemporary British poetry. The tone of the poem, building as it does on an earlier piece like 'I.M. David Penhaligon', is far from the type of work that won Maxwell most praise in the 1990s. One hopes that he will be able to consolidate this without abandoning the other, wilder possibilities which poems like 'Deep Song of Us' and 'Once Was, Is Now' suggested. If not he runs the risk of spending the rest of his career turning out the self-repeating poems that make up most of the collection. But 'My Grandfather at the Pool', 'Cap D'Ail' and some work that has appeared recently in journals suggests the prospects are good.

*For the record, my list is as follows: *Tale of the Mayor's Son* (1990): 'Tale of the Mayor's Son' , 'Mr Gem' , 'How Many Things' , 'Select' , 'Poisonfield' , 'I.M. David Penhaligon' , 'London from My Window' , 'Once Was, Is Now' ; *Out of the Rain* (1992): 'Errand Boy' , 'War Hero' , 'We Are off to See the Wizard' , 'The Day After Christmas' , 'The Fires by the River' , 'EC3' , 'The Eater' , 'We Billion Cheered' , 'One and Another Go Home' , 'Helene and Heloise' , 'Deep Song of Us'; *Rest for the Wicked* (1995): 'The Sarajevo Zoo' , 'Ost' , ' The Altered Slightly' ; *The Breakage* (1998): 'My Grandfather at the Pool' , 'Letters to Edward Thomas' #12, 'Cap D'Ail' .

Editor's note: This article was written before *The Boys at Twilight* (Bloodaxe), a selection of Maxwell's first three books, was published.

JO SHAPCOTT

Like Sean O'Brien, Jo Shapcott was one of the writers virtually certain of a place in New Generation who was denied it on the grounds of the promotion's own-goalish age limit. Since then she has consolidated her position with a vengeance, winning the Forward Prize in 1999 for *My Life Asleep*, her last book from Oxford University Press. The demise of the Oxford Poets list was not as serious for Shapcott as for many others because Faber quickly issued a collection of her first three books: *Her Book* (1999). The anthology she co-edited with Matthew Sweeney, *Emergency Kit*, helps define her *ars poetica* in its stress on transformed experience rather than empiricist recording. Her work is acutely aware of all the registers of language available to the poet and the politics that lies behind choosing one register rather than another. John Kinsella has said that she is "doing no less than rewriting the English poetic canon".

PEGASUS
after Rilke

Every girl's loved a horse once, as fiery as Pegasus,
his gallop, his breathy run, even the full stop
hers. Mine punctuated the air with hooves, crushed
the earth underneath until it exploded into water.

I was always waiting for Pegasus, ready to dabble
fingers in the sparks which gushed from his hoof-prints.
Can you feel how the sweetness tries to master you?
How your neck is learning to be curbed by flowers?

THE FOURTH LIE
after Rilke

You say: I dreamt, and not: I lied.
When you wake up, it's a strange bed.
You open the door, shamefaced,
on a room so devastated

you run for the lift to the ground floor.
It tings, says, "Doors closing".
There are lies flying in the air
utterly grey from living upside down.

THE NATIVITY STORY
after Rilke

What could three Magi
bring to the party?
A little bird in a cage,
an enormous key

from a far-off realm
and the balm
my mother used to buy
made from strange lavender

which grows only round here.
You mustn't speak ill of these shreds.
They were enough to turn my child
into God.

The Shape-Shifter

JANET PHILLIPS INTERVIEWS JO SHAPCOTT

I'd like to start by asking you about early influences. In an essay in Contemporary Women's Poetry *you talk about almost meeting Elizabeth Bishop, in 1979, while you were at Harvard. Could you tell us a bit about that time?*

I'm interested in the way any reader, me included, strikes up friendships with writers they never meet (who may be dead, after all!). And I suppose we don't think enough about the standpoint of the reader. For a reader, a writer (dead or alive) who engages them can become a very profound friend – or enemy, or lover – it is, after all, a very intimate relationship. It's not just the books that move into your house, it's the writers too: you talk to them, argue with them, tussle with them. For me, Bishop was one of those figures.

At the time I was devastated not to meet her [Bishop sadly died soon after Shapcott arrived in Harvard], but I think in retrospect I'm probably glad. I did see her read, however. Her voice was much deeper than I'd anticipated, a very musical contralto. No wonder she mentions music so often in the poems – from Baptist hymns to bird song – and the sound world she makes is so rich, so deft.

You were at Harvard on a scholarship – was that to study a particular subject?

There are gangs of poets who, when they're young, think they want to be straightforward academics but almost certainly don't! In those days, I was writing a PhD about Bishop and was awarded a Harkness Fellowship to go to Harvard for two years. I was allowed to take any courses I wanted, from Latin to History of Science, and beyond. And I did. I followed up my research, too: I went to Vassar, for example, to look up Bishop's papers there. But I was at Harvard the first year Seamus Heaney taught there and by the end I was doing nothing but writing and more writing.

What was it like, being able to take classes with Seamus Heaney?

I was very lucky to have such a mentor at just that moment. And by total accident, too! I was also taught "versification" by Robert Fitzgerald, a fine poet and translator of the classics. He was just about the scariest man you could imagine. We had to do a weekly exercise on the form that he had lectured on the week before, and he would project our exercises on to the wall and critique them. The best grade you could get was "ntb": not too bad.

Being in the States was important to me as a developing writer. I think it made me a different kind of poet. It gave me a confidence about what I was up to which I wouldn't have had if I'd stayed here. That was the 'seventies when there weren't as many published women poets here whereas in the States it felt much more open. Later, when I was well into my second book, *Phrase Book*, I went back to America (my brother moved there) seeking something I needed for the shape and sound of my new poems. To do with momentum, speed and pacing. To do with the vertical movement of the poem as well as the horizontal movement across the line. Something I wasn't hearing at home.

Unfortunately there's a perceived dichotomy between people who practice free verse and people who practice traditional form, which is sometimes unhelpful. Most of the poets I admire do both, very naturally, and will fall into whatever they need for a particular poem. But early in my career, free verse as it was practised here was often not great: it tended to be flat, dull, lazy. I felt there were more interesting versions of it in the States. I'm not sure that's true any more but it was then.

Besides Harvard, you have held fellowships at Cambridge and the British Library, and you were Northern Arts Literary Fellow from 1998-2000. Does a poet have a natural place within a university?

I was Judith E Wilson Fellow at Cambridge – an important time for me. I'd been working full-time as an arts administrator at the South Bank, devising education programmes around arts events there, a job which I loved, but I was working hard, long hours, with little time to write (although I did publish my first book of poems while I was there). On the plus side, my job gave me the chance to mix with composers and musicians – I learned a huge amount from that. But Cambridge gave me time to finish *Phrase Book*, and think and read.

I don't know whether the university is a natural place for a poet or not. At the moment I'm visiting professor at the University of Newcastle which I like, not least because it gives me a foot in such a vibrant place – Newcastle is a real centre for poetry. We've a new MA there called Writing Poetry, with poets like Ian Duhig teaching.

At Cambridge I came across a strand of poetry new to me then, and was fortunate enough to meet a whole spectrum of poets I hadn't read before. I loved the idea of a poetry scene in which no one cared what publisher liked what, or who the audience was, or how many of them there were. It was important to be reminded to focus only on what can we wring out of this language of ours. A breath of fresh air.

Do you think work by women poets gets judged differently, that some critics can't separate the woman from the writing and will always describe it in terms of how "feminist" it is? When you won the Forward Prize for My Life Asleep *in 1999 the judges described it as being "full of post-feminist triumphalism". Is that an accurate assessment for you?*

I don't know what it means! When you read things like that – and it's probably better not to read them – it feels like it's not about you. But people can say what they like – you have to let the work go to that extent. But coming back to women and the scene here, there are loads of wonderful women writers now. What interests me is that although we've moved into a new century we're still using our old eyes. We're used to looking back and hunting out big testosterone monoliths: Chaucer, Wordsworth, Hughes, Heaney. You're looking for them, your eye wants to identify them, because that's what we've always understood as literary history. But maybe it's just different now that there are all these women. In the end, you still look for those writers who will move in with you.

Who are the writers who have moved in with you? Apart from Bishop, you've also written a poem to Dennis Potter. Are there others? A sheaf of unsent letters to literary figures?

My next book is a love letter to Rilke. It's called *Tender Taxes* – coming out this autumn. It's a collection of poems which began when I started reading Rilke's poems in French. He wrote over four hundred of them. I was intrigued by the idea of Rilke – another great monolith, maybe? – casually, or so it seems, deciding to write in another language. And it does bring out a different side to him. He's frothier, still metaphysical, still spiritual, but lighter. I think I must be quite perverse: I'm doing versions in English of the work of a poet who's writing in a different language from his own – how mad is that?

I began looking at these poems and writing what at the beginning were versions and then quickly became responses, or sometimes arguments, or sometimes dramatisations. I can't find the word for what they are – versions isn't it. Bunting coined the term "overdrafts" but that's not quite it, in this case, either. In some of the poems Rilke appears – he walks through them. But in each case, my poem has a parallel poem in one of his. I never intended these versions to be a book – it started because I liked the poems, and it was one of those things I enjoyed picking up every now and then.

You've published versions of Rilke's Windows *before, in* Phrase Book, *and* The Roses *appear in*

My Life Asleep. *Are these part of the book?*

There are four sections in the book, two of which have been published before. In 'The Windows', the first section, Rilke has created a character in a room, looking at the walls, the furniture, the windows and a woman, who comes into the picture sometimes. The poems are very introverted but once I started thinking about how you might look through a window or look at it, I arrived quickly (as I'm sure Rilke intended) at matters of God. And I tried to translate *The Windows* quite straightforwardly at first. But I couldn't make his language work in my own. For example, he addresses the windows: "O Windows" – which sounds impossible to my ear. So I started to dramatise the poems. I thought: I've got to change the voice, the voice doesn't work. Who would be in a room talking to the windows? I decided it was a man (still), probably drunk, and lonely, so the character I invented to speak the poems is a bit like Philip Marlow the detective, sitting alone in a room – but still with a touch of the metaphysical, still Rilke at heart. And that's how the first sequence came about.

The second sequence is called 'The Roses'. Rilke's version consists of twenty-seven tiny little poems, each of them a different rose. I realised when I was well into this that in fact they were probably twenty-seven different girlfriends, and more than that, twenty-seven different sets of female genitalia – but by then it was too late, I was committed to the project! And just like in *The Windows*, he addresses them. So, for example, he might say: "O Rose, you are like x or y or z". My poems turn the perspective round, the roses speak, they disagree "It's not like that, it's like this". But they're still love poems, in my versions, still pungent. I think maybe it's an extended love poem to Rilke, himself.

The third section is pastoral. Rilke wrote a group of poems called *The Valaisian Quatrains* at a time when he was in the country with his lover, Balandine Klossowska. I think maybe for him the French language is associated with this particular woman, and with love. Their correspondence was conducted entirely in French. And in fact *The Windows* was first published together with illustrations by her (she was an artist) – you could see it as a kind of joint love project. I spent ten years hunting for that particular edition – having not seen the illustrations – then I discovered internet bookshops, found it on the web at once and in less than five days the book was in my hands. Having seen it, I wonder if he wrote the poems from her sketches rather than the other way round.

Rilke's version of pastoral is strange. In pastoral you expect death – the grit in the oyster, mortality: *et in Arcadia ego*. At the very least the perspective of the city is allowed to give shade to the otherwise golden light. But Rilke's pastoral avoids darkness. His movement might simply be, for example: from mountains, to beauty, to God. No grit, death, no shimmer of difficulty at all. That was mind-boggling. His poems are set in Muzot, in Switzerland, a place I didn't know at all, so I've moved them somewhere familiar to me – to the Welsh borders. In my poems Rilke appears as a character, he walks in and out of them, and we talk to each other. My versions are much darker.

The sequences are divided by five poems about lies. There's something about the whole book being a hunt for the truth, how it was, how it seems now and how difficult it is to say what anything is, at any one time. About the hunt for permanence when there isn't any, for things being fixed when they can't be. And gender, of course. In any history of women's writing you read of women being over-written or written out, so perhaps, in *Tender Taxes* – though it didn't start this way! – there's an inkling of the reverse. Writing back to Rilke feels more audacious than it should.

Is there a particular quality in Rilke's writing that's got you hooked?

Well, there's lots, but what Rilke and Bishop have in common is transcendence. Almost every poem is an epiphany. They're never writing just about what you see. Bishop was keen to capture in poems what she calls "the mind in action" and the movement of that mind, for her, had to be towards some other goal, so it's never writing as mere self-exploration, it's exploring matters to do with the world around, society perhaps, and then to do with God – but both poets do it in ways that are rooted first in the material.

I get the sense from your work that you want to avoid personal history and to embrace the contemporary world, what's in the news, or even in the future. Do you think poetry is slow to do this, compared to other artforms?

That's a really interesting idea. Have you read the notebooks of Leonardo Da Vinci? He homes in on this. He's trying to compare the merits of the different art forms and, of course, for him, the visual arts come out on top. He implies that painting is superior to music because it has all of its history there, in the moment. It's something you apprehend in real time, but all of its history and all of its future lives there in the moment of apprehension. Whereas music is linear, you have to live in it and pass through it in time. I got interested in this notion because what it doesn't take into account is the accumulation of images, even in music, the memory of the other moments. I wonder whether poetry has all of it: the image, the moment and the memory of what's gone before.

But that wasn't what you asked me. I guess I've always felt that novelists have more freedom than poets to explore the lives of others. People expect poets to write about themselves and their history. Even when it's not about you, they'll read your poem as if it is. Novelists are allowed to make things up and take things anywhere they want. I love that freedom. In my writing there's lots about boundaries and different skins and different worlds. It may be that I feel the self is enclosing, and I like the idea that you can pass out of it, and get into other places, other imaginations, other skins.

I wanted to ask you about the animals – I know that's not particularly what you're doing at the moment. But it's one of the things you are known for, the poems about sheep and goats and the Mad Cow...

I don't think there are any animals in the new book – oh, apart from a horse. I suppose I like the idea of inhabiting other skins, you can pretend you have a different sensibility, and test what that might be like, against yourself. Having said that, though, my animals are quite cartoon-like. I don't pretend to be telling precisely what it's like to be that sheep on that hillside. My poems go somewhere else, say more about humanity than about the life of a sheep (I hope). It's no co-incidence that I like beast fables, I love Chaucer. Tales that are both moral and animal. Tales that deal with shape-shifting and the poet as that kind of shape-shifter – which is why the myth of Thetis is so appealing to me. As for the mad cow herself – like everyone else I watched the television coverage where they kept running the same clip of this poor animal staggering and falling to her knees, but to me her eyes seemed terribly wise. I suppose the mad cow in my poems is a holy fool. And of course women sometimes get called "You mad cow" and I wanted to transform the insult, to make the affront a positive thing in her.

Emergency Kit *and* Last Words *are two anthologies you have worked on. Could you explain the ideas behind each one?*

Emergency Kit *was a gift to do. We didn't have to put together one of those summing up books which*

seeks to explain and sell one vision of what poetry in the twentieth century might be – who's in, who's out. Both Matthew Sweeney (co-editor) and I wanted to collect poems for people who were new to poetry, poems that would excite them and that would make them want to read more. We collected from the whole world – with the proviso that every poem should be written in English first. That gave it a very particular flavour – it wasn't at all limited geographically. Matthew always called it the weird second cousin of *The Rattlebag*.

Last Words (edited with Don Paterson) was different because every single poem was newly commissioned. It emerged from a poetry festival we were involved with, in Salisbury – one that had no poetry readings. Instead of readings, poems were specially written to be placed around the city of Salisbury for a week, for example, in delicatessans, in shoe shops, to be tattooed, to thrown across the sky in fireworks: it was wild but fun.

What did you think of the New Generation promotion in 1994?

If it made people buy more books and think more about poetry, which I suspect it did, it was a good thing. But it wasn't an actual "thing" – probably my colleagues who were in the New Generation would agree that, in reality, poets get together more spontaneously to do things, discuss things, so having a "pastry cutter" from outside outlining "a movement" probably doesn't have much impact on the poets, although it could do on the public. From the inside out, I don't think the poets would recognise themselves as a cohesive group. Susan Wicks wouldn't turn to Jamie McKendrick and say: "We're a movement".

Which contemporary poets are you reading now?

I thought about this question before I came. I thought, you know, I'll be asked who I like. Names of various poets, of course, flooded into my mind. And, no question, I do think we're living at a vibrant moment for poetry – I've read almost everything published this year and was unexpectedly heartened. Then I thought to myself, well, this sort of question has little tags attached to it. One way in which the poetry scene has become mean is that the names you mention are used to define you. As if there can be no such thing as simply celebrating what you love. Your choices flag up something about yourself, where you fit in, how good you are, what school you're in. So I thought I wouldn't answer. The thing for me, as always, is that I want to get away from these boundaries.

CAROL ANN DUFFY

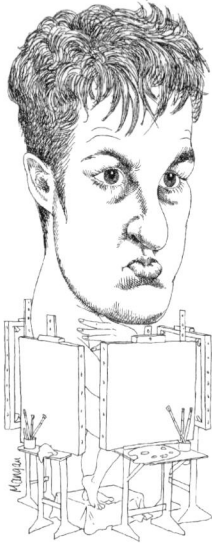

The figurehead of New Generation who decided at the time she'd rather stay at home, Carol Ann has vindicated the faith people had in her then by becoming an indisputably popular poet alongside Heaney. The poet's poet in 1994, she is quite clearly now the People's. One could dispute whether *The World's Wife* is a better book than *Mean Time*, her collection at the time of New Generation but it clearly has what most poetry books lack: an overriding theme, a memorable title, a real reason to exist. She has had a model career, gaining momentum with each book. Since her move to Manchester and motherhood she has been happily productive, publishing two excellent collections of poetry for children (*Meeting Midnight*, Faber, 1999; *The Oldest Girl in the World*, Faber, 2000), has edited the anthologies *Time's Tidings* (Anvil, 1999) and *Hand in Hand* (Picador, 2001), and for young people, *Stopping for Death* (Viking, 1997). She is currently a recipient of a National Endowment of Science Technology and Art (NESTA) award – a fellowship for work in progress. *The Laughter of Stafford Girls High* is from her next book *Feminine Gospels*, due from Picador in Autumn 2002.

from THE LAUGHTER OF STAFFORD GIRLS' HIGH

. . .

Five minutes passed in a cauldron of noise.
No-one could seem to stop. Each tried holding
her breath or thinking of death or pinching
her thigh, only to catch the eye of a pal,
a crimson, shaking, silent girl, and explode
through the nose in a cackling sneeze. *Thank you!*
Please! screeched Miss Dunn, clapping her hands
as though she applauded the choir they'd become,
a percussion of trills and whoops filling the room
like birds in a cage. But then came a triple rap
at the door and in stalked Miss Fife, Head of Maths,
whose cold equations of eyes scanned the desks
for a suitable scapegoat. *Stand up, Geraldine Ruth.*

Geraldine Ruth got to her feet, a pale girl, a girl
who looked, in the stale classroom light, like a sketch
for a girl, a first draft to be crumpled and crunched
and tossed away like a note. She cleared her throat,
raising her eyes, water and sky, to look at Miss Fife.
The girls who were there that day never forgot
how invisible crayons seemed to colour in
Geraldine Ruth, pale face to puce, mousey hair

suddenly gifted with health and youth, and how –
as Miss Fife demanded what was the meaning of this –
her lips split from the closed bud of a kiss
to the daisy-chain of a grin and how then she yodelled
a laugh with the full, open, blooming rose of her throat,

a flower of merriment. *What's the big joke?*
thundered Miss Fife as Miss Dunn began again
to clap, as gargling Geraldine Ruth collapsed
in a heap on her desk, as the rest of the class
hollered and hooted and howled. Miss Fife strode
on sharp heels to the blackboard, snatched up
a finger of chalk and jabbed and slashed out
a word. *SILENCE*. But the class next door,
fourth years learning the Beaufort Scale with Miss Batt
could hear the commotion. Miss Batt droned on –
Nought, calm; one, light air; two, light breeze; three,
gentle... four, moderate... five, fresh... six, strong breeze;
seven, moderate gale... Stephanie Fay started to laugh.

What's so amusing, Stephanie Fay? barked Miss Batt.
What's so amusing? echoed unwitting Miss Dunn
on the other side of the wall. *Precisely what's*
so amusing? chorused Miss Fife. The fourth years
shrieked with amazed delight and one wag,
Angela Joy, popped her head in the jaws of her desk
and bellowed *What's so amusing? What's so*
amusing? into its musty yawn. The third form
guffawed afresh at the sound of the fourth
and the noise of the two combined was heard
by the first years, trying to get Shakespeare by heart
to the beat of the ruler of Mrs Mackay. *Don't look*
at your books, look at me. After three. Friends,

Romans, Countrymen . . . What's so amusing? rapped out
Mrs Mackay as the first years chirruped
and trilled like baby birds in a nest at a worm;
but she heard for herself, appalled, the chaos
coming in waves through the wall and clipped
to the door. Uproar. And her Head of Lower School!
It was then that Mrs Mackay made mistake number one,
leaving her form on its own while she went to see
to the forms of Miss Batt and Miss Dunn. The moment

she'd gone, the room blossomed with paper planes,
ink bombs, whistles, snatches of song, and the class clown –
Caroline Joan – stood on her desk and took up
the speech where Mrs Mackay had left off – *Lend*

me your ears . . . just what the second years did
in the opposite room, reciting the Poets Laureate
for Miss Nadimbaba – *John Dryden, Thomas Shadwell,*
Nahum Tate, Nicholas Rowe, Laurence Eusden, Colley Cibber,
William Whitehead, . . .but scattering titters and giggles
like noisy confetti on reaching Henry Pye as Caroline Joan
belted out Antony's speech in an Elvis style –
For Brutus, uh huh huh, is an honourable man.
Miss Nadimbaba, no fan of rock'n'roll, could scarcely
believe her ears, deducing at once that Mrs Mackay
was not with her class. She popped an anxious head
outside her door. Anarchy roared in her face
like a tropical wind. The corridor clock was at four.

The last bell rang. Although they would later regret it,
the teachers, taking their cue from wits-end Mrs Mackay,
allowed the chuckling, bright-eyed, mirthful girls
to go home, reprimand free, each woman privately glad
that the dark afternoon was over and done,
the chalky words rubbed away to dance as dust
on the air, the dates, the battles, the kings and queens,
the rivers and tributaries, poets, painters, playwrights,
politicos, popes . . . but they all agreed to make it quite clear
in tomorrow's assembly that foolish behaviour –
even if only the once – wasn't admired or desired
at Stafford Girls' High. Above the school, the moon
was pinned like a monitor's badge to the sky.

Miss Dunn was the first to depart, wheeling
her bicycle through the gates, noticing how
the sky had cleared, a tidy diagram of the Plough
directly above. She liked it this cold, her breath
chiffoning out behind as she freewheeled home
down the hill, her mind emptying itself of geography,
of mountains and seas and deserts and forests
and capital cities. Her small terraced house looked,
she thought, like a sleeping face. She roused it
each evening, kisses of light on its cheeks
from her lamps, the small talk of cutlery, pots

and pans as she cooked, sweet silver steam caressing
the tender rooms of her home. Miss Dunn lived alone.

So did Miss Batt, in a flat on the edge of the park
near the school; though this evening Miss Fife
was coming for supper. The two were good friends
and Miss Fife liked to play on Miss Batt's small piano
after the meal and the slowly shared carafe of wine.
Music and Maths! Johann Sebastian Bach! Miss Batt,
an all-rounder, took out her marking – essays on Henry VIII
and his wives from the Fifth – while Miss Fife gave herself up
to *Minuet in G*. In between Catherine Howard
and Catherine Parr, Miss Batt glanced across at Fifey's
straight back as she played, each teacher conscious
of each woman's silently virtuous love. Nights like this,
twice a week, after school, for them both, seemed enough.

Mrs Mackay often gave Miss Nadimbaba a lift,
as they both, by coincidence, lived on Mulberry Drive;
Mrs Mackay with her husband of thirty-five years,
Miss Nadimbaba sharing a house with her aunt
and Aphra, a Siamese cat. Neither had ever invited
the other one in, although each would politely enquire
after her colleague's invisible half. Mrs Mackay
watched Miss Nadimbaba open her purple door and saw
the cat rubbing itself on her calf. She pulled away
from the kerb, wondering if Mr Mackay fancied fish
for his meal. They had nearly completed the crossword;
Mr Mackay calling out clues – *Kind of court for a bounder* (8) –
while she got out Roget, Brewer, Pears, the OED.

The women teachers of England slept in their beds,
their shrewd or wise or sensible heads safe vessels
for the Wife of Bath's warm laugh, Othello's jealousy,
the phases of the moon, the country code;
for Roman numerals, Greek alphabets, French verbs;
for foreign currencies and Latin roots, for logarithms, tables,
quotes; the meanings of *currente calamo* and *fiat lux* and *stet*.
Miss Dunn dreamed of a freezing white terrain
where slowly moving elephants were made of ice.
Miss Nadimbaba dreamed she knelt to kiss Miss Barrett
on her couch and she, Miss Nadimbaba, was Browning
pleading *Beloved, be my wife* . . . and then a dog began to bark
and she woke up. Miss Batt dreamed of Miss Fife.

U A FANTHORPE

U A Fanthorpe was famously a late-starter in poetry, beginning at the age of fifty after a career in teaching and then a spell (very productive for her poetry) as a hospital receptionist. Since then she has been prolific with seven books from Peterloo and a Penguin *Selected Poems*. In her most recent books, *Safe as Houses* (Peterloo, 1995) and *Consequences* (Peterloo, 2000), her poetry deals increasingly with what it means to be English in a time when old certainties have collapsed: "So in us, The high-rise people and the dispossessed, / The telly idols, fat men in fast cars, / Something reverts to the fine dangerous strain / Of Galahad the Prince, Lancelot the Undefeated, / Arthur the King". In 'Counting Song', from *Safe as Houses*, cardboard-city dwellers are seen as: "...the heirs, the true Londoners, / Who work in this stern meadow. The others / are on their way to somewhere else".

SECRET GARDEN

There's no such thing. Gardens are never secret.
If a single swan (as here) complacently
Inverts itself on a lake, then at once another
Shows up, thrumming its way through air. One human
(As here) in a garden means another somewhere,
Categorizing umbelliferae,
Transmitting a therapeutic kiss, or in search of a cutting.

Then there's the infiltrators. Artists omit them.
But consider the endlessness of worms, the manic
Engineering of moles. Serpents, of course,
Famously get into gardens. And if the painter
Had had more room for sky, there'd surely have been
Some gull drifting over, taking a bird's eye view.

The genuine secret garden is suburban,
A couple of cupfuls of sour clay, wrenched
From railway embankments and ring-roads,
Where every grassblade's cut by hand. No robin ventures
For fear of leaving a claw-mark.

However high their walls, all gardens
Are open cities. And, as astronauts know,
All the world's a garden. All the men
And women jobbing gardeners, discouraging green.

Leave any tarmacked scrap for a moment, and something
Comes quietly through: ivy, grass, bramble,
The great first-footers. Other feet, too.
A fox may winter out in that potting shed,
And lovers know how to climb over orchard walls.
As, if she's lucky, here.

JONSON AT HAWTHORNDEN

(Drummond speaks*)

He must have left a lick of himself behind,
After that famous twenty-stone trudge from London.

Endless infallible views of the man who knows
All about everyone (most of it damaging):

Shakespeare lacked art; Sidney was plain; Petrarch
A blackguard for over-production of sonnets.

I wasn't exactly unnerved. But he kept on.
He'd killed his two men, twice done time in the Clink –

There's a clutch of eminent mortal enemies after him.
He'll write, he says, about his visit here.

He calls himself The Poet. I'm
Too good and simple, it seems. Would

Be wise to give up on poetry. Won't excel.
And yet this bin of flesh, this brawling bully

Writes O such sweet and O such tender verse.
He is the nonpareil he says he is,

But God be praised, he's gone. I'll write my comment
(*A great lover and praiser of himself*)

Then pace my paths, and listen to my rooks.
Rude swaggerers, they have a touch of him.

*Jonson came to Hawthornden in the summer of 1618, and seems to have left in early January 1619. See the enormously entertaining Conversations, *noted down by Drummond, who says nothing at all himself.* Ben Jonson, *ed. Donaldson, OUP, 1985.*

KATE CLANCHY

Kate Clanchy is one of the most prominent of the new wave of mostly women poets who have emerged post-New Generation. She acknowledges Carol Ann Duffy's help and influence but her poetry is mostly her own. Many of the poems in her first book, *Slattern* (Chatto and Windus, 1996), were poems of transient relationships evocatively realised ("There was not enough between us / to keep a cat alive" – 'Towards the End'). *Samarkand* (Picador, 1999), on the other hand, features a section of poems of homemaking, 'The NewHome Cabaret', with a house pared down to "the best spare modern style" and bits of the unspare, ancient style emerging from the cracks (a 1954 *Daily Mirror* headline – 'Modern Housewives' War on Dust'). The last poem neatly twins settling down and transience: "We live here now.../ We are the lights / the trains flick by in the dark".

ANEURYSM

When my father heard his friend
was dead, we sat a while and talked
of traffic: how cars clog
every by-way now, every road
you think you know. We were quiet,
and I lit the lamp. I thought

I could hear the cars outside,
bashing, lowing, rank on rank.
There'd been a crash, my father said,
and his friend had walked out,
shaken, saved. It was hours
before the blood-clot got him.

I held my baby on my lap. It was
dark, dark, the winter solstice.
We said there is no such thing
as the right route or a clear passage
no matter where you start,
or how you plan it.

THE BURDEN

I'd never have thought that this would be me,
content to tote the baby homewards
answering, rook-like, his hoarse calls,
counting the haws on the bare claw branches,
the rose hips shining like blood.

and you'd be the one at the gate left staring
at clouds cross-hatched on the burnished water,
the flooded fields we couldn't cross.
That I'd let a hundred yards stretch between us.
How bright this thin, bisected, moon.

ANDREW MOTION

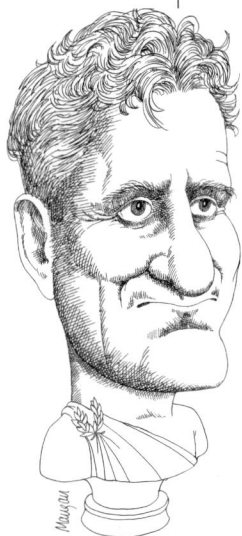

When Andrew Motion was merely in contention for the Laureateship
rather than its incumbent people wondered why, of all the possibles, he
was the only one who actually seemed to really want the job. We now
know why. He is not only already the most effective Laureate in living
memory but he is a better poet too. It is as if he knew he needed such a
context in which to function at his best. The contrast with 1994 is
dramatic. Then he was derided by the editors of the Bloodaxe *New
Poetry* as a representative of a discredited Oxbridge hegemony and he
was just outside the frame of New Generation, having been born in
1952 (it is also unlikely the judges would have selected him had he been
eligible). While poetry was touted as the new rock 'n roll, his profile was
low. Now he is the most ubiquitous poet in the country, constantly on
radio and TV: an ambassadorial role that suits him perfectly. His latest
collection is *Selected Poems 1976-1997* (Faber, 1997). His Laureate
poems are yet to be collected.

THE MESSAGE
In Memory of Sarah Raphael

1.

A crystal mid-winter Saturday dawn
and the names of things the same

as things themselves: flash-over frost
sealing my garden-square; the ash tree

perfectly matched by its ghost in mist;
unshakeable hush through the street.

I take it all in as I climb the stairs
to my room, completely at home

yet free as a bubble in water,
wanting for nothing except

the handful of change and jacket I need
before I go out to the world.

And here on my desk is the toad-head
jewel in my telephone winking.

Why should I answer it now? This moment
is mine. But I do. I answer it feeling

the terror which started inside me
a lifetime ago, and that's how I hear

you are dead. The peaceable street;
the ash in its trance; the frost.

These all look exactly the same. What's new
is the crash of them splitting apart from their names.

Not, you, Sarah. Not you.

2.

I rang your number
and heard your voice
on the answerphone –
un-deliberate grace

in a message-rush,
and your hasty fall
on the word "good-bye",
though you were well

when you set it down
and never knew
how it might endure,
outliving you

like the travelling light
of a snuffed-out star
cascading to meet
the ignorant stare

of us below,
who blink and look
and are not sure
which things to take

in our little mist
of breath-by-breath
as signs of life
and which of death.

3.

In your telephone
the tape has been changed, and now the glib machine
remembers only a new regime.

In your desk
a tidy number of unopened letters lie
bearing your name and the brand of missing days.

In your studio
the bubble-cartoons of all your brilliant ideas
have reached the ceiling, and stuck, and will not stir.

In your children's room
the spine of a favourite book is aching to bend
open and let the story end.

HUGO WILLIAMS

Hugo Williams was once corralled with Ian Hamilton and Colin Falck as a member of a new generation of Post-Movement minimalists. Williams' work has survived several stylistic sea changes in the body-poetic since then with élan. In *Strong Words*, he commends the plain and simple – "If it doesn't look easy, your aren't working hard enough" (Fred Astaire) – and his poetry relies very heavily on charm, a beguiling narrative style allied to colourful subject matter – his own life. His latest book, *Billy's Rain* (Faber, 1999), has been his most successful, winning the Eliot Prize. Williams has perfected a direct buttonholing style, seen at its best in the popular anthology poem 'Prayer' from *Dock Leaves*: "God give me strength to lead a double life". He often poses rhetorical questions that lead the reader straight in to the writer's life: "Do you think I mind..."; "How do you think I feel..." His treatment of sex is mordant, and often hilarious; "When it's time to go to bed in one of my lives . . . / Tell me this: do I wear pyjamas here, / or sleep with nothing on?"

EGG AND SPOON

Look out! Look out!
Here come the parents, the mad delivery boys,
holding out to us in spoons
the sum of all they know.

Their eyes pop out of their heads,
they bite their tongues,
in their efforts to place something
infinitely precious in our mouths.

THREE-LEGGED RACE

Hobbled with a handkerchief, out of step,
heaving off in opposite directions,
pulling each other down,

it's obvious to anyone looking on
this isn't their event, never could be,
and yet they feel inclined to take it seriously.

Arms round one another's shoulders,
necks stretched out in concentration,
they take a few steps in unison

before losing it again. They pick themselves up
and hurl themselves forward once more
in the general direction of the finishing line.

You can tell from the expressions on their faces
just how close they think they are
to getting the hang of it at last.

MICHAEL DONAGHY

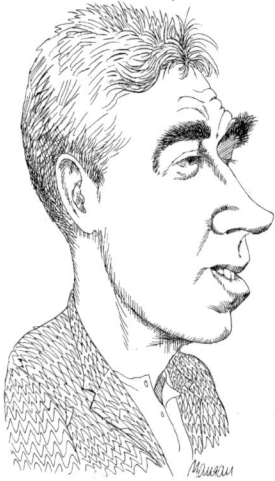

Michael Donaghy is the most consistently formal poet of the current generation. He generally writes in metre and stanza and his models are the American old-formalists: Hecht, Wilbur, Merrill (he has little time for the New Formalist movement) with MacNeice in there somewhere. His work aims at lyrical perfection and has got stronger with each book, a trend happily recognised by the success of his third collection, *Conjure* (Picador, 2000), which won the Forward Prize and picked up several Books-of-the-Year recommendations. Donaghy is often fictively inventive, as in 'The Palm', a mystery fantasy concocted around the idea that Django Reinhardt and Paul de Man were in the same Cannes hotel in 1942. 'Quease', from *Conjure* is a *tour de force* of blurred identity and could do for self-consciousness what Les Murray did for 'Sprawl': "Quease builds a portaloo about itself, / a lift that takes one passenger, then drops".

SOUTHWESTERNMOST

I've a pocketwatch for telling space,
a compass tooled for reckoning by time,
to search this quadrant between six and nine
for traces of her song, her scent, her face.
Come night, that we might seek her there, come soon,
come shade the southwest quarter of this chart,
the damaged chamber of my mother's heart.

Mare Serenitatis on the moon,
this blindspot, tearhaze, cinder in the eye,
this cloudy star when I look left and down,
this corner of the crest without a crown,
this treeless plain where she went home to die.
I almost hear it now and hold its shape,
the famine song she's humming in my sleep.

FROM THE SAFE HOUSE

I can just see Claire your good wife reading you this.
It has arrived this morning at your orchard in Vera Cruz
where your four brown daughters hector six chickens
and you lie beneath the dusty blue pickup
tying back the exhaust with a rusty hanger,
getting ready for the long haul north.

There are parts she skips, parts about her.
And parts I've yet to write or find a way to write.
The paper she reads from is yellowed, sharp creased,
badly typed, postmarked Chicago, decades late,
from a Reagan winter, Pax Americana for Grenada,
the coldest winter of the life of the mind.

Soon I'll climb through snowdrifts to post it
from our clapboard commune on the South Side
on a night six mummies dug from permafrost
huddle in coats breathing clouds in a room of books
watching the last chair leg gutter on the grate
towards the heat death of its universe.

But for now it's still flickering, and Claire is beside me.
I'm too cold to talk, too cold to think, except of her.
I hear you hammer the ice from your boots on the porch.
and the door slams back and you blow in from Urbana
from over the lake, from marching with steelworkers,
and make the first move to the shelves.

Four highlighted copies of *One Dimensional Man*,
old phone books, Jaws, *The Sensuous Woman by J*
She's the first shovelled in to the fire. You find it now,
hidden behind her, mimeographed, its staples gone to rust,
urgent and crumbly as this letter Claire's holding:
the *Manual of the Weather Underground.*

We'd been a safe house since '68 and never knew.
Did the Feds? Claire lets go my hand, takes it from you
and sniffs *Could it be any colder there?*
Lit by flaring paperbacks and tequila she reads us,
like a bedtime story, the drill for escape.
I enclose it, with some photos of my son.

I have sent them you *then*, to the farm you planned,
to the heat haze in which you seem to waver,
where you lie beneath the same unsteerable wreck
your wife taught me to drive when you were drunk
and which I still own a seventh of, let's not forget,
(Tell him we never slept together, Claire)

instead of *now*, when I hear of your death,
after your stroke at my age give a month or two,
now, when you never made it to Mexico
and Claire remarried and never had children
and the clapboard safe house fell down at last
and the blue pickup went for scrap years back.

Charming Armani

by Ian Sansom

MICHAEL DONAGHY

Dances Learned Last Night
Poems 1975 – 1995

Picador, £7.99
ISBN 0330 481 940

Conjure

Picador, £7.99
ISBN 0330 391 10 0

HERE COMES SWANK, said Dennis Skinner famously of David Mellor. Well, here comes swish:

> Dearest, note how these two are alike:
> This harpsichord pavane by Purcell
> And the racer's twelve-speed bike.
> ('Machines')

Note the slight cock of the head and the inclination towards intimate address ("Dearest"). Note also the natural force, the guiding hand on the elbow ("note"). Note the purse of the lips in the recherché vocabulary ("pavane"). And note the slight smirk running from dimple to dimple, from Purcell to the twelve-speed bike. Let me introduce you: Michael Donaghy.

Donaghy is the winner of the latest Forward Prize for Poetry, for his third collection, *Conjure*. He is therefore officially the smartest kid on the block. He is *summa cum laude*, a gentleman and a scholar, and a metaphysical shnook. His characteristic mode of address – firm and familiar, eager to please – echoes throughout his first two collections, *Shibboleth* (1988), and *Errata* (1993), now collected and repackaged by Picador as *Dances Learned Last Night*. The beckoning can first be heard in the poem 'Pentecost' ("See? It's something that we've always known") and continues on through 'Pornography' ("And remember that time") and on into 'Acts of Contrition' ("There's you"). Donaghy's poems are clearly not unaware of their attractions. They've got it, and they know how to flaunt it: "I've had an important dream. But that can wait" ('Analysand').

In *Conjure* there's no let up in the charm offensive – "Yes I know its not funny" ('Timing'). If anything, he's added a few nods and winks to the practised shrug, the glad-hand and the wide open smile. The opening line of 'The Pallace of Memoria Garnished with Perpetuall Shininge Glorious Lightes Innumerable', for example, sounds uncannily like the two women in Woody Allen's Catskill resort hotel: "It's shut. And after such a climb!" Where would we be these days without bathos? Indeed, the best, the smoothest, opening in the new book has Donaghy sounding like something between Allen's trademark bumbling nebbish and John Berryman's Henry: "Can I come in? I saw you slip away. Hors d'oeuvres depress you, don't they?" What comes across strongly here, as in all of Donaghy's poems, is the charismatic power of a person.

It can hardly be said often enough: Donaghy's poems charm. Charm can of course be off-putting: people who can turn it on are usually a turn-off. Virtuosity can be an obstacle to intimacy, which is why the great poets can sometimes seem cold and distant, making out with language like Alex Comfort's beardy free-lover. In a sentence, as in a suit, you need a few crumples. One thinks – doesn't one, just – of Anthony Powell's Peter Templer, "there was always a slight impression that he was too well dressed", and there is in Donaghy's earlier poems a slight impression that he is too well read: the creases are a little too sharp. He seems sometimes to arrive at a profundity by too short a route, or out of context. Some poems read like the *Very Best of Simone Weil*, or, say, *101 Uplifting Thoughts for Those Dark Nights of the Soul*: "The machinery of grace is always simple" ('Machines'). "Though we command the language of desire, / The voice of ecstasy is not our own" ('Pentecost'). The authority is not always earned, and sometimes the observations seem hardly worthwhile: "And the stars we think we see on moonless nights are long extinguished" ('The Present'); "Desire attained is not desire" ('Deceit'). Uh-huh.

But if these few examples make the poems sound shiny and hollow it should be pointed out that Donaghy works hard to fill them out and achieve a structured elegance – a kind of verse Armani. He seems to be striving to achieve a kind of timelessness – and most of the time he carries it off. His method seems to consist of recovering moments and incidents and holding them up to the light:

Let's hold the sad toy storms in which we're held,
let's hold them gingerly above the bed,
bubbles gulping contentedly, as we rock them to
               sleep,
flurries aswim by our gentle skill,
their names on the tips of our tongues.
                ('Our Life Stories')

Much of his work consists of such tiny worlds brought to life, his poems like crystal balls filled with flitter:

Musicians in the kitchen, Sunday morning in
                Gweedore.
An American with a tape recorder and a yellow note
                book.
"What was the name of that last one?"
The piper shrugs and points to the dark corner.
"Ask my father".
The American writes "Ask My Father".
         ('The Natural and Social Sciences')

The angels have come early for the miracle.
They've gotten into the bar and drunk it dry.
Grinning, staggering, shedding feathers,
They can barely stand up, let alone fly.
                ('A Miracle')

Even when he's not constructing these miniature *mise en scènes* he's busy rigging up an amusing little ship-in-a-bottle. In the new poem 'Local 32B', for example, the narrator tells the story of how when he was working as a doorman on the Upper East Side he once got a cab for Pavarotti: "Yessir, I put the tenor in the vehicle". I bet you didn't see him pull the string to hoist the sails on that one.

In *Conjure* Donaghy seems to want to lay bare the workings of his magic, to reveal his techniques, to flash his rather exquisite lining and to confess to all his careful double-stitching and seamings. 'Caliban's Books', begins "*Hair oil, boiled sweets, chalk dust, squid's ink ... /* Bear with me. I'm trying to conjure my father". In the simple, magnificent first poem in *Conjure*, 'The Excuse', a poem about his father, Donaghy shows the reader the hidden wires which animate the whole collection, and you suddenly realise that for all the show and all the bluster, and for all the flirtations and talk about desire, his work is really about dependence, dependents, and attachment:

But if
I had to rig up something, and I do,
Let my excuse be this, and this is true:
I fear for him and grieve him more than any,
This most deceiving and deceived of men ...
Please hang up and try again.

Conjure is very good. "Conjure" is perfect: from the Latin conjurare, "to band together by an oath, to charm, and to call upon".

How Many 19th Century Poets Have You Read?

by Tim Kendall

The Bloodaxe Book of 20th Century Poetry from Britain and Ireland

Ed. Edna Longley

Bloodaxe, £10.95
ISBN 1 85224 514 X

ANTHOLOGIES, BEN SONNENBERG has argued, are interesting only in proportion to their exclusivity. Proof has come in recent years with the predictable glut of calendar-inspired overviews, all covering slightly different periods with slightly different agendas, and all brim full of the great, the good and (predominantly) the utterly forgettable of twentieth-century poetry. Hiding behind buzz-words like "pluralism" and "democracy", these anthologies claim to provide a rich harvest which is in fact little more than the product of their editors' unwillingness or, in some cases, inability to make intelligent value judgements.

Edna Longley observes no such restraint. Advertising her relatively narrow selection, the blurb declares that she has omitted "showy, noisy, ephemeral writers who drown out their contemporaries but leave later or wiser readers unimpressed". (Quite what her publisher, Bloodaxe, makes of this is open to speculation.) Unlike several of her predecessors, Longley has no shopping list of gendered, regional or ethnic poetries to tick off. As she has devastatingly contended before, "Considerable metropolitan careers have been built upon perpetual marginality". Longley's guiding principle, we learn, is "aesthetic precision". Even so, she includes fifty-nine poets in her anthology – parsimonious compared with her competitors, but far more than the mid-twenty-first century will bother reading. And there are some startling absentees: no Housman and no Kipling (both of whom wrote much of their best poetry after 1900), in an anthology that finds room for John Hewitt. No David Jones. And no Betjeman, whose 'Death in Leamington', at least, deserves inclusion. But denouncing sins of omission is a favourite sport among reviewers, and Longley, despite her exclusivity, has less to repent than most anthologists.

Reviewing anthologies by Armitage / Crawford and O'Brien, Longley finds both guilty of "fragmentation". In each, well over one-third of the poets are represented by a single poem. Longley smells cowardice, imagining the editorial dilemmas: "Can we leave her out after the *Poetry Review* hype?" (*Poetry Review*, seen as home to the fashion-conscious if not the fashion victim, is an easy target for Longley's sniping.) With the exception of a four-page chunk of Bunting's *Briggflatts*, Longley avoids single-poem authors. This allows distinctive voices the time to clear their throats; it becomes possible to tell what poets sound like, and to form judgements on whether they are worth all the attention. Major figures have around ten pages, and Longley's emphasis on the lyric ("This anthology is essentially an anthology of twentieth century lyrics") ensures that they average a poem a page. Longley does not pretend that we can fully appreciate a poet's style on the basis of ten poems; but those poems, together with the few hundred words of introduction given to each poet, do provide a valuable basis for further exploration. On the whole, Longley selects very well, although she does sometimes have a tendency to ignore a poet's later work: *Four Quartets* goes virtually unmentioned; there is nothing from Hughes after *Moortown*, nor from Hill after *Tenebrae*; almost all of Muldoon comes from his first four books. And once or twice, a conspicuous absence reflects an age-old and still raw controversy: Longley, like Muldoon before her in his *Faber Book of Contemporary Irish Poetry*, omits the bog poems in Heaney's *North* altogether. Like it or not, this is what Longley has called elsewhere "a properly opinionated canon", committed, vibrant and courageous.

Longley's heroes – she has very few heroines – will be obvious enough to those who have read her published criticism. Her touchstones are Hardy and Yeats, the two "poles of her Anglo-Irish dialectic" (to re-direct her own words on Larkin). In Housman's absence, chronology fortuitously dictates that they should appear at the head of her anthology. Edward Thomas has long benefitted from Longley's brilliant advocacy, but without her ever quite dispelling the suspicion among sceptics that he is being overpraised for strategic reasons. However, the fun starts when Longley tackles modernism which, aside from Eliot, barely gains a foothold in this anthology. Longley grits her teeth in the introduction to acknowledge "the huge impact of *The Waste Land*", only to redeem her position three lines later by announcing that Eliot's poem "has been canonised by academic criticism in a way that may overrate its formal influence". The biggest gainers are the war poets (Second as well as First) and the generation from Northern Ireland which came of age in the 'sixties and early 'seventies. Derek Mahon, for example, receives more space than Ted Hughes or Sylvia Plath, although Longley cannot bring herself to include more than one short poem from his recent work.

Longley's serene course through the canon becomes gradually bumpier as she approaches the present day. She foresaw the problems in her essay 'The Millennial Muse', an overview of twentieth-century anthologies recently collected in *Poetry and Posterity*. There she notes that anthologies "tend to collapse in a lottery of names when the 'new' impends". Very few younger poets win prizes in Longley's lottery, but the lucky ones do seem to have been chosen at random. After the last indisputably major poet, Paul Muldoon (born 1951), Longley accommodates six others: Jo Shapcott, Ian

Duhig, Carol Ann Duffy, Kathleen Jamie, Simon Armitage and Don Paterson. None of these is an entirely laughable or inappropriate inclusion, but neither do any of them have a body of work (to date) which evidently deserves representation.

Longley's choices raise questions which she nowhere seeks to answer. Why, for example, Kathleen Jamie and not Lavinia Greenlaw? Shouldn't room be found for Michael Hofmann? Is Jo Shapcott really a better poet than Craig Raine? Is Longley not privileging those poets – Duhig, Armitage, Paterson – who belong to the school of Muldoon? That these debates are endless proves Longley's problem; after the inevitable march of great names her anthology collapses into the provisional and contingent. Longley decides not to invest heavily in any of her six poets; none has more than six pages. Theirs is, of course, work in progress; yet the seven pages (not enough?) awarded to Keith Douglas, dead at twenty-four, serves to illustrate Longley's reservations about the current generation of young poets. Shapcott's experiments "seem designed to discover emotional truths", Duffy's "poetry readings are extremely popular". With praise like that, Longley effectively announces a rollover.

LAVINIA GREENLAW

Lavinia Greenlaw's one book at the time of New Generation, *Night Photograph* (Faber, 1993) established her reputation as a coolly original poet who was drawn towards scientific subject matter, or at least narratives of the lives of people touched by Science. She was poet-in-residence at the Science Museum from January to August 1995. Her second book, *A World Where News Travelled Slowly* (Faber, 1997) is a book of restlessness, journeys with a new partner, observed *à la* Elizabeth Bishop, dazed nights ("The city is baked and blown by incontinent weather") and days in which armadillos are encountered. 'Guidebooks to the Alhambra' is one of her most characteristic poems, twining the personal and some fairly arcane lore ("Where the rusted fountain was evidence // of the murder of the Abenceragas cavaliers"); this poem also contains the *leitmotif* line, "Things change, become home and we must leave them", and the kind of enigmatic ending that is typical not just of her poetry but of much poetry written today: "Even Irving...knew it had to be iron oxide". She received a grant from NESTA in 2000. Her first novel, *Mary George of Allnorthover* (Flamingo) is reviewed on p. 40.

THE SPIRIT OF THE STAIRCASE

In our game of flight, half-way down
was as near mid-air as it got: a point
of no return we'd fling ourselves at
over and over, riding pillows or trays.
We were quick to smooth the edge
of every step, grinding the carpet to glass
on which we'd lose our grip.
The new stairs were our new toy,
the descent to an odd extension,
four new rooms at flood level
in a sunken garden – a wing
dislocated from a hive. Young bees
with soft stripes and borderless nights,
we'd so far been squared away
in a twin-set of bunkbeds, so tight-knit,
my brother and I once woke up finishing
a conversation begun in a dream.
It had been the simplest exchange,
one I'd give much to return to:
the greetings of shadows unsurprised
at having met beneath the trees
and happy to set off again, alone,
back into the dark.

Quietly Shattering

by Elaine Feinstein

LAVINIA GREENLAW

Mary George of Allnorthover

Flamingo, £12.99
ISBN 0 00 710595 9

LAVINIA GREENLAW IS a distinguished poet with an unusually musical ear, known particularly perhaps for the witty use of people from the history of science and her ability to imagine their lives, though the range of her achievement is far wider. Inventing stories, then, and taking on a cast of voices other than her own is hardly a new departure. Nevertheless, this ambitious novel represents a startling expansion of her talents. Mary George is a seventeen-year old schoolgirl growing up thirty years ago in a small East Anglian village. She is an engagingly eccentric heroine, whose difficulties in handling her contact lenses are as tenderly evoked as her clumsy sexual fumblings. The other inner world the novel explores is that of Tom Hepple, recently released into the community from a hospital that has been treating him for mental illness. Tom is drawn back to Northover where his dead mother Iris once lived, though her old house is now lying under the lake in Inglewood Dip, where it can still be made out through the water.

A troubling web of secrets bind the families of the Hepples and Georges together, for it was Iris Hepple who took Mary's father away from her mother Stella, and it is Matthew George who inherited Iris's house, or at least the money paid in compensation for its flooding. It is perhaps to signal these many links that Tom sees Mary when he returns as an angel able to walk on water, while Mary is afraid of him, as if sensing all the hatred and spite the novel gradually uncovers. The novel is set in the 'seventies, in a summer of water shortage, oil crisis and power cuts. What makes it a poet's novel, in the best sense, is the richness of the texture. I am not thinking here only of the period detail, nostalgic for anyone who can still remember the arrival of punk rock, and that summer of drought and petrol shortage; nor even the sensitivity to fen landscape. What is impressive is the vigour of the language, and the solidity such energy brings to human portraits. Mary, coming home after her first all night party is dressed awkwardly in an old dress and hand knitted string cardigan; the Scout discos and jumble sales that make up a social life in rural East Anglia are at once drab and unpredictable, coloured by adolescent sexuality. Greenlaw writes brilliantly of a young girl's first experience of desire, the sense of air on exposed flesh as a skirt is lifted, the heady mix of fear and excitement.

Novels and poems have moved towards one another in our time, so that mood in both genres can depend on a shimmer of surface detail and the rhythms of a particular voice. Here, the writing is sometimes suffused by that inexplicable adolescent happiness which can co-exist with pain: "The rain had just stopped, and the sun was still a low pink light that suffused the wet houses with a foreign rosiness and made leafless branches shine". This is a lyrical note Greenlaw allows herself only occasionally. From the opening of the novel, everything is physically very real: ugly smells – the stink of burning tyres, ammonia and diesel – suffuse the air around Inglewood Dip. The water shortage produced by the drought means that Mary has to take a bath in the cloudy bathwater left by her mother, whom she often bitterly resents, even though she shares her misery at her father's desertion. Greenlaw has a sharp eye for human gesture: the "cramped movements" of people used to living in caravans for instance, and she can give a cruelly surreal portrait of the face of an ageing woman, seen upside down at the hairdresser's where Mary shampoos customers on Saturdays. "Her pulled back hair revealed a line where her foundation ended in a tidemark... Mary imagined peeling it off like a mask... saw the tiny knot of veins throbbing at her temple and the thick corded veins among the crumpled skin of her neck".

For most of its length this novel has an elusive, magical quality as if it belonged to a lost age, as well as inhabiting a landscape notoriously cut off from the rest of England over the centuries. Yet under the golden haze there is always menace. Tom is handsome and seemingly gentle, lost in memories of his sick mother, and the tubes that sustained her while she still lived at home; caught up in his dream of the past village. But his gentleness can be provoked, and the conclusion of the novel is both tragic and violent, only saved from outright melodrama, indeed, by Greenlaw's wonderful control of tone.

SEAMUS HEANEY

Seamus Heaney's career has consisted of a series of peaks, each apparently unsurpassable at the time. After the Nobel Prize he might have been expected to coast a little but he had something up his sleeve. It is easy to see how *Beowulf* (Faber, 1999) was a brilliant project for him, less easy to see how it became a runaway best-seller. The timing was obviously right: in Heaney's translation *Beowulf* becomes a head movie of a world as brutal as ours but in a different way; as an Amazon reviewer puts it: "Heaney does, in a few hundred lines of translated verse, what many 'best selling' fantasy authors fail to do – this just grabs you by the throat and shakes you till you listen". His new book *Electric Light* (Faber – reviewed on p. 43) and the poem here show him returned from the Dark Ages to a more genially celebratory and valedictory mode in poems with a strongly classicised feel.

POSTSCRIPT TO ST. LUCIA

March, the lion, paws the sand
Of Sandymount. The famous strand
Ineluctably rejoices
As scudding gusts and tidal noises

Rise up to where I sit and write
At home behind my attic skylight,
Far from Castries and Gros Islet,
Vieux Fort, Soufrière and Rodney Bay,

Far from *en bas gorge* and steel
And catamarans on double-keel,
The morning swim, the sunblocked doze,
The urge to throw off *all* the clothes,

Far from our beach-head barbecues,
(Those little deep-fried *balahoos*)
And vinous, long verandah lunches
And ruddy sunsets with rum punches.

Dear host and hostess of St. Lucia,
Re-work the spell, return us to you!
It's as if in distance set between us
Your fabulous, far *locus amoenus*,

Your Prospero-rough-magicked dream
Of cloud-capped *piton*, cove and stream
Grew insubstantial, hazy, weak
As our sometime glimpse of Martinique.

Torquoise, green and blue, the sea
Was water-water-coloury:
My first paint-brush and box of paints,
My childhood's puddly wash and tints –

That primal reach for the more of art –
It reawakened in my heart.
Under the palms and *Bois-canot*,
Like a punch-drunk Douanier Rousseau

I lounged, luxuriated, drifted.
Tectonic plates inside me shifted.
Ice-caps melted. Global warming
(O most benign and unalarming)

Entered the body and the soul.
My tropics stretched from pole to pole.
Earth and Eden mingled there
As in a mural by St. Omer.

Yet earth it was, and no mistake.
I loved the life, the give and take,
The stalls of fruit, the roadside rumshops,
And cows in swamps, and crowds at bus-stops,

The breadfruit, the banana plant,
Helonica and *flamboyante* –
Not to mention booze at *Buzz*,
The ice-cold vodka's frigid fuzz,

Marie's whiskey sours, and lyric
Beverages prepared for Derek,
All recorded by S. Nama –
"Hold it! Hold it! Where's the camera?"

So from the wind-whipped Dublin shore
I walk back towards the open door
Of the studio, its siesta calm
And breathing-space, the light's *I am*

In which once more I settle, sit
For one last touch-up to the portrait,
Sit, drift, hold the pose and stare,
Not sure if I am here or there.

Peat Smoke and Byzantium

by Harry Clifton

SEAMUS HEANEY

Electric Light
Faber £7.99
ISBN 0 571 20798 7

ANYONE, AS PATRICK KAVANAGH wrote, can sympathise with failure – but it takes a great saint to sympathise with success. The same poet also wrote, in a late lyric:

No, no, no, I know I was not important as I moved
Through the colourful country, I was but a single
Item in the picture, the namer not the beloved....

So what do you do when, like Seamus Heaney, you are both the namer *and* the beloved? When your special dilemma is to exist between the eggheads and dons with their classical knowledge, and a common reader like the one here in 'Glanmore Eclogue', for whom words like "Cumae" and "Heracles" are dead spots in a poem, and who asks for an understandable song? When you ended your last *Collected Poems* with a perfect lyric and are yearning for new ways forward, a looser box of tricks? When, after thirty years of quasi-public utterance, the personal past you were sidetracked from seems as remote and pastoral as Arcadia? When the ghosts of Plato and William Yeats come whispering What Then? *Electric Light*, explicitly, implicitly, tries in its tentative way to address those questions.

This, it is worth remembering, is really the first Heaney collection since *Door into the Dark* (1969) not backlit by conflagrations on the Falls and Shankill. Which offers an opportunity, beyond the political immediacies of the intervening years, to get back to the poet's childhood, boyhood, youth in the 'forties and 'fifties, and the world, already slightly classicised ('Helicon', 'Undine') of the earlier poetry in the 'sixties, and to take up the misplaced thread of a story there that resumes itself in the present. Instead of Dante's hell, P.V. Glob's bog-excavatings, Mandelstam's and Sweeney's inner emigrations or Milosz's historical ironies, the genii are Moscus and Bion, with a nod to John Clare, the Virgil of the *Eclogues*, and the pipings of a latter-day Lycidas in a version of pastoral that is the Bann Valley:

Bann Valley Muses, give us a song worth singing,
Something that rises like the curtain in
Those words *And it came to pass* or *In the beginning*.

Help me to please my hedge-schoolmaster Virgil
And the child that's due. Maybe, heavens, sing
Better times for her and her guardian.

('Bann Valley Eclogue')

The stylised discourse, the deliberate archaism *à la* John Crowe Ransom's "antique harvesters" will, as it were, divide the sheep from the goats. Those who agree with Yeats that "Rhetoric is the will doing the work of the imagination" will not like it. Those who feel, with Eliot and Montale, that rhetoric has its place, will take it on board. Either way, a pre-lapsarian mid-century mid-Ulster is evoked, incubating the tensions and explosions of later decades, a Golden Age of fixity-in-flow eels and perch, of boarding-school days and home births overseen by Asclepian doctors with Hygeia to hand, and the gradual onset of civicly rational if not Hellenising electric light that gives the book its title. Arcadia, then, but shot through with the subterranean rumblings of the IRA border campaign in the 'fifties, a harbinger of what is later to come.

> There is I believe, a "Heaney moment", an invocation of chthonic forces not so much threatening as existing alongside human life, as its id-self or its non-human "other". The true terror of these forces, unlike interhuman evil, is that they are morally neutral.

Soot-streaks down the courthouse wall, a hole
Smashed in the roof, the rafters in the rain
Still smouldering;
      When I heard the word "attack"
In St Columb's College in nineteen fifty-six
It left me winded, left nothing between me
And the sky that moved beyond my boarder's
      dormer...

All very well in its way, but the classicising agenda, it has to be said, has a heavy air of contrivance. The evocations of a past world of sepia-tinted innocence fed to the threshing-machine of contemporary politics are top heavy with mythic self-consciousness, "as if" analogy. An *ex post facto* attempt to Balkanise this Northern Irish anterior world, via the Struga Poetry Festival of 1978, and steal a piece of East European political relevance along the way, is far too clever for its own good:

In Belgrade, I had found my west-in-east

('Known World')

Bernard Henri-Levy, the fly-drive French *philosophe* still wiping off the egg left on his face by Sarajevo poets, could have saved him that particular trouble. But Heaney, too, is a creature of his age, a liberal humanist age of intellectual guilt, concern and helplessness, poetically postmodern, where sheer or mere connectedness, and the more heterogeneous the elements the better, is an end in itself. Dante and the Gaeltacht, Beowulf and the Border Campaign, Asclepius and the local G.P., the cross-pollinating of Heracles, Hardy and Michael Collins in 'The Loose Box'. It is literary depth of field rather than any silent mystical reality lying or not lying behind the poem that is expected to underwrite its authenticity.

A special case in all this is 'The Augean Stables', one of six 'Sonnets from Hellas' which chart the poet's travels through that luminous classic world while referencing out to more contemporary matter:

And it was there in Olympia, down among green
      willows,
The lustral wash and run of river shallows,
That we heard of Sean Brown's murder in the
      ground
Of Bellaghy GAA club. And imagined
Hose-water smashing hard back off the asphalt
In the car park where his athlete's blood ran cold.

It stands out, partly due to the high-risk high intensity fusion of Art and Life more loosely thrown together elsewhere in the volume, and partly because it is public utterance, the enunciation of a proper name in an enlarged context. Not accidentally perhaps, that larger context is not only Greek but American, the pages of the *New Yorker*, where this poem appeared a year ago, the Olympus not of poetry but of power.

Hellenisings apart, the rest is the struggle with that intractable given of the English tradition, the pentameter blank verse line. Heaney has gone back as far as Coleridge's "conversation poems" –

Well, they are gone, and here must I remain,
This lime-tree bower my prison!

— and fast-forwarded through his own 1974
take on that in the 'Singing School' sequence –

Well, as Kavanagh said, we have lived
In important places, times.

– to get to a chatty, colloquial line that stays
squarely in the middle range of feeling and remi-
niscence, and works by accumulation rather than
short-winded intensity, an ingathering of appar-
ently casual matter that adds up to more than the
sum of its parts. The Thomas Kinsella of *New
Poems 1973* is somewhere behind it too, but really
it is Patrick Kavanagh's "true note on a dead slack
string" that is the sought-after effect, especially in
'The Real Names', which rings changes on the art
and life theme as it remembers school-fellows from
St Columb's, in and out of their Shakespearian
roles.

House lights down
Liam McLelland enters, Ferdinand
Sleepwalking to the music, spied upon
By Gerry O'Neill cloaked up as Prospero.

This, like much else in the same vein, hovers
dangerously between Kavanagh's ideal and Auden's
"just reeling off their names is ever so comfy". The
pentameter line has always tended to convention-
alise and flatten out Heaney's best effects, which
grow, as he rather exasperatedly acknowledges in
'The Fragment', like side-effects from the middle
of a poem:

"Since when" he asked
"Are the first and last line of any poem
Where the poem begins and ends?"

Ted Hughes, one of the elegised dead in the
book's second section, has mentioned a quintessen-
tial "Shakespeare moment". There is also, I believe,
a "Heaney moment", an invocation of chthonic
forces not so much threatening as existing along-
side human life, as its id-self or its non-human
"other". The true terror of these forces, unlike inter-
human evil, is that they are morally neutral. They
range from the "slime kings" and "eels like hatched
fears" of the first collections, through the well-
known "fungus plump as a saddle" in *Field Work*,
to the pure gravitational power of 'The Weight' in
his last book – though only the first part of that

latter poem, since the second moves hastily to tame
and civilise it with an ingratiating overdub. There
is one such moment in *Electric Light*, as the boy
Heaney steps into the sea near Portstewart:

In the deep pool at Portstewart, I waded in
Up to the chest, then stood there half-suspended
Like Vitruvian man, both legs wide apart,
Both arms out buoyant to the fingertips,
Oxter-cogged on water.
My head was light,
My backbone plumb, my boy-nipples bisected
And tickled by the steel-zip cold meniscus.
('Vitruviana')

That "steel-zip cold meniscus", where the whole
indifferent universe laps ticklingly against the "boy-
nipples" of the human, is Heaney at his quietly
deadliest. It is not a strength he plays to, in this
collection. A shortened line, a heightened register,
might have brought it about more often.

I have avoided, so far, any mention of the
dreaded N-word. But what recipient of that award
cannot have looked over his or her shoulder at the
fabulous aftershower of poems granted to Yeats in
The Tower, and wished for something similar? This
book is not and was never intended to be *The Tower*
(his last collection, the 'Mycenae Lookout' poems
especially, are closer in spirit to the later Yeats), but
it does nevertheless, in its low-mimetic late twenti-
eth century way, keep Byzantium on the radar
screen.

What George Mackay Brown saw was a drinking
deer
That glittered by the water. The human soul
In mosaic. Wet celandine and ivy.
Allegory hard as a figured shield
Smithied in Orkney for Christ's sake and Crusades,
Polished until its undersurface surfaced
Like peat smoke mulling through Byzantium.
('Would they had stayed')

Peat smoke and Byzantium, the Gaelic local and
homely over against the golden kingdom of Art.
Isn't that too the central tension of *The Tower*, with
its id-instinctual flux and its glittering fixities? No
need to insist though, and the best poems in this
uneven, transitional collection do not. The master-
switch of Attic light shows simply an old woman
knitting.

PAUL MULDOON

Paul Muldoon is the Houdini of modern verse, the poet most admired by the younger poets, much imitated despite the risks. *The Annals of Chile* (Faber, 1994) won the T. S. Eliot Prize and contains both his most accessible long poem, 'Incantata', an elegy for the artist Mary Farl Powers, and one of his most baffling free-association extravaganzas, 'Yarrow'. Of *Hay* (Faber, 1999), Muldoon's last collection, Rod Mengham said: "Muldoon's remodelling of the languages of religion and politics is occasionally magisterial but more often impish, the terraforming of an environment in which protocols and formulae of all kinds are repeatedly twisted out of shape, but never so far as to lose their critical elasticity". In *Hay,* Muldoon's 'sixties roots emerge in a series of poems about rock music: 'Sleeve Notes', while 'The Bangle (Slight Return)' is a series of Wallace Stevensish sonnets inspired by a meal in a Parisian restaurant. *Poems 1968-1998* is published by Faber in May.

THE OTTER

That was the year S– – told him how on the Queen's desk
there lay a great six by four foot blotter

of such a blackness, she would aver,
a blackness so dense

and a grain so close, so compact,
no one could hope to hold

a mirror up to it
and thereby hit

on any evidence of clandestine contracts or covenants, of old
enemies having entered a secret pact

to which she might be a party or affix her hand, any evidence
of the treachery he now saw written all over her,

rising as she did to meet him like the otter
that had risen that time to meet him from Lough Eske.

MICHAEL LONGLEY

Michael Longley has been on something of a roll in recent years after a lean spell in the 'eighties when the poems weren't coming. *Gorse Fires* (Secker, 1991) was followed by *The Ghost Orchid* (Cape, 1995) and *The Weather in Japan* (Cape, 2000), which won the T. S. Eliot Prize. In all three books Longley mines a vein of delicate description that is indeed often Japanese in its precision and poise. Longley's poetry relishes texture, both in the world – he often writes of voluptuous fabrics – and in language: he is drawn to the vowel music of Greek flower names: "asphodel", "anemone"; he is in fact the most musical of contemporary major poets. Longley is a cherisher of things, wrapping them in a rich burr of sound colour. The delicate touches in his poetry are often literal touches, as in 'The Ghost Orchid': "Just touching the petals bruises them into darkness".

THE PATTERN

Thirty-six years, to the day, after our wedding
When a cold figure-revealing wind blew against you
And lifted your veil, I find in its fat envelope
The six-shilling Vogue pattern for your bride's dress,
Complicated instructions for stitching bodice
And skirt, box pleats and hems, tissue-paper outlines,
Semblances of skin which I nervously unfold
And hold up in snow-light, for snow has been falling
On this windless day, and I glimpse your wedding dress
And white shoes outside in the transformed garden
Where the clothes-line and every twig have been covered.

AN OCTOBER SUN
in memory of Michael Hartnett

Something inconsolable in you looks me in the eye,
An October sun flashing off the rainy camber.
And something ironical too, as though we could
Warm our hands at turf stacks along the road.

Good poems are as comfortlessly constructed,
Each sod handled how many times. Michael, your
Poems endure the downpour like the skylark's
Chilly hallelujah, the robin's autumn song.

TOM PAULIN

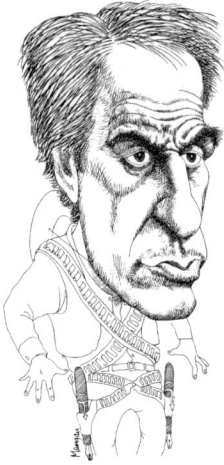

Tom Paulin's writing entered a new, prolific phase with *Walking a Line* (Faber, 1994) which continued with *The Wind Dog* (Faber, 1998). His early work was tautly political, sometimes imitative of East European models, but the new style was free, unbuttoned, using many coined words to convey the improvisatory nature of thought. In *Walking a Line,* he is like Lawrence in trying capture the essences of things in free verse. In *The Wind Dog* the poems often proceed by free association, rather as Paul Muldoon's do: in the title poem "cargo cult" leads him to Masefield's poem and then via the word "cheap" to the "clishclash" of "cheapo rings on a curtain pole". The improvisatons of Paul Klee and the highly coloured vernacular of Chagall are important inspirations in his recent work. In 2000 he was awarded a NESTA grant to complete a long poem about the Second World War. The first volume, *The Invasion Handbook* will be published by Faber in Spring 2002.

THE YELLOW SPOT

We can see them still
lingering over a late lunch
in the Savoy Grill
though this time
it's the Ritz
– they're both in blue pinstripes
that look a shade chalky
– I've a hunch
that dry as dust texture
has to be exactly right
as they chew – Montgomery Belgion
a lightweight a nono who likes
the term *cathedratic*
as they chew Monty Belgion
and Tom Eliot
a knotty even a gristly
point – theology or politics –
no Tom says God is not a shout
in the street
most definitely not
– quite so says Monty
I know of course which Irish lout
said that – the same who put the Jew Bloom
inside his new green Jerusalem

of course Tom replies
I admire his well yes
his Jesuitical intelligence
but we must find some substitute
for that type of sense
it tends rather much to travel
though it could
of course be transported
to somewhere cold
– strange how everything comes back
to poor Coleridge's caves of ice
they're every bit as fated
as a railway track
– can I entice
you? says Monty reaching for the bottle
he completely fails to notice
a slight rictus of displeasure
on the face of his companion
who turns the subject to Byron
the church cat
suede shoes how awful
(does he not know I wear them
wonders Monty?)
– of course Arnold Tom says
was a mere savage
in a tone that's jaunty
the ever suave – or at least suede – Monty
says yes Arnold
might've been better on the stage
as a nigger minstrel

over coffee Monty
quite by accident singes
his winedark moustache
as a match manages to miss
his cigarette
– quick now
he puts it out
but for a long drawnout moment
like a breach of etiquette
they catch a bony a bristly pong
that might be a bad poem
or a worse song

trying to make a statement
– then not to embarrass
each other they play a favourite game
and try to come up – yes come up –
with a rhyme for *Ritz*
no not *Biarritz*
murmurs Tom if we test our wits
there must be some place some name
far away to the east
– maybe you can tell me what fits?

Half a Stone of It

by David Wheatley

The New Penguin Book of English Verse

Ed. Paul Keegan

Penguin, £20
ISBN 071 39921 07

"NORMALLY THERE IS no class of book more slip-shod, more boring, more prejudiced, more snob-bish, more exclusive, more incestuous, more narrow-minded, more arid, more ignorant, more canonical, more soulless, more soul destroying, more anti-poetic than a poetry anthology", wrote Paul Durcan. Forty-five years after John Heyward's first stab at the title, Paul Keegan's *New Penguin Book of English Verse* hardly qualifies as "normally" by anyone's standards of anthology-making. But while this majestic new tome easily sees off the rest of Durcan's slings and arrows, one word isn't so easily got around: "canonical". The average slim volume is as loosely connected to the canon as St Pancras Station is to St Pancras: just as you don't need to know who that gentleman was to hop on a train, the total canonical picture isn't something you expect to swim into view when you pick up a single book. Yet here it is, one thousand, one hundred and thirty-nine pages and half a stone of it: the English canon.

"History has many cunning passages, contrived corridors / And issues", said Eliot's Gerontion, and the question of how best to thread a path through them is highlighted by Keegan's inspired decision to organise this book by date rather than author. There are immediate advantages to this. For a start it inhibits the compass-and-ruler, who's-got-the-most-pages approach to anthology reviewing, which can only be a good thing. Secondly, it takes poems out of their usual backdrop of an entire career trajectory telescoped artificially into a couple of pages. No longer can the Coleridge of 'Duty Surviving Self-Love' (1829) camouflage himself against 'Kubla Khan', or Yeats the 'nineties poet pack-hunt with the Nobel laureate and the mad old man. Keegan arranges things like a good party host, making sure all his guests are talking, and not just to themselves. Where in the past it's been easy for Eliot to stand apart from the First World War poets, it's less so when we find 'The Love Song of J. Alfred Prufrock' and 'Aunt Helen' sandwiched in between Edward Thomas and Isaac Rosenberg, with *The Waste Land* still twenty-five pages away. Instead of swallowing all of Hardy in one lump before returning to Hopkins, Bridges and Henley, we find him bobbing up all over the place, between Wilde and de la Mare, H. D. and Yeats, and Joyce and Austin Clarke. And that's just the nineteenth and twentieth centuries. There are troublesome cases, where composition and publication dates vary wildly or poems exist in different versions; these are signposted with the relevant dates in brackets and without much damage to the overall pattern. Suffice to say that Traherne's 'Wonder' appears under 1671 rather than 1903. Yet even without these considerations, the vagaries of chronology throw up interesting patterns. After Hardy's 'The Darkling Thrush' in 1900 nothing happens until Walter de la Mare's 'The Birthnight' in 1906, whereas the six years from 1916 to 1922 yield thirty-seven pages, from Lawrence's 'Sorrow' to Gurney's 'The High Hills'. How would contemporary poets feel at the thought of a future anthologist selecting exactly nothing from all the books published in the last six years?

No less predictably than anthologies with the word "British" in the title, books of "English Verse" raise obvious and weighty questions of who and who not to put in. Just what does that adjective mean? The Anglo-Saxons? Sorry, not English. Hayward fixed Tottel's 1557 *Songes and Sonettes*, the first anthology of recognisably modern English verse, as his point of departure and started with Wyatt; Keegan opts for the fourteenth century. The Scots? After the shocking omission of Burns from Hayward's book, at last yes, with representatives from three of the many languages in which Scottish poetry can be found (English, Scots and Gaelic). The Welsh? Again, at last yes, though R. S. Thomas's 'Gifts' ("from my sad country the shame") characteristically loves and curses its Welshness at once. And the Irish? Yes please, even at the risk of another verse letter protest from Seamus Heaney. Robert Crawford and Mick Imlah's recent *New Penguin Book of Scottish Verse* kicked off with an Irishman, St Columba, and Keegan does the same with 'Ich am of Irlande'. His youngest authors, in fact, in the pleasingly hibernocentric closing stretch of the book, are Paul Muldoon and Nuala Ní Dhomhnaill, the latter, as so often, misspelled yet again.

Which just leaves the English. When it comes to the great central plain of the book, from the Elizabethans to the Victorians, Keegan trumps Hayward comprehensively. The stretch where we move from Wordsworth and Coleridge through Byron and Shelley to Keats in particular is superb (Keegan gives 'The Eve of St Agnes' in its entirety as the first of Keats's seven poems for 1820). It's also safe to say that among Keegan's favourite poets

are Herbert, Fulke Greville, Marvell, Lovelace, Campion, Johnson (always an anthologist's favourite, for some reason), Dryden and Swift. But here are William Diaper, Abel Evans, Joseph Skipsey, Amy Levy, May Kendall, Adelaide Anne Procter and Anna Wickham. There is a large tally of epitaphs and elegies in this book, but as these examples show, after Hayward's more parsimonious approach, there are resurrections too.

If there is any area where we find Hayward putting in writers that Keegan omits, it is the twentieth century. Gone are Francis Thompson, Lionel Johnson, Masefield, Edith Sitwell, Day Lewis and Spender. Despite its blithe dismissal of Irish, Scottish and Welsh verse, Hayward did succeed in bucking the Anglocentric trend of *Oxford Book* editors Sir Arthur Quiller-Couch and Dame Helen Gardner to include a dozen odd Americans from William Cullen Bryant to e. e. cummings. Even with no apparent ban on its presence however, Commonwealth verse failed to get into his book. Keegan imposes just such a ban, and restricts himself to three London-based Americans, Pound, Eliot and Plath.

For Hayward, ballads, dramatic verse and poems in dialect were out. In his 1998 *Oxford Book of English Verse* Christopher Ricks broke with tradition to include dramatic verse, though restricting himself to Elizabethan and Jacobean. Keegan does not follow suit here, but is surely right to tear down the *cordon sanitaire* that kept 'Tom o' Bedlam's Song' and 'The Twa Corbies' out of his predecessor's pages, though I think he has missed a chance by including 'Johnny I hardly knew ye' over the more scarifying 'The Night before Larry was Stretched'. Some of the most agreeable surprises in Keegan's book come not just from the balladeers, but the even more invisible territory for past anthologists of public inscriptions, such as the following from St Mary Magdalene Church in London: "Grass of levity, / Span in brevity, / Flowers' felicity, / Fire of misery, / Winds' stability, / Is mortality", and this self-reflexively hourglass-shaped example from Osmington in Dorset:

> Man is a Glas: Life is
> A water that's weakly
> walled about: sinne bring
> es death: death breakes
> the Glas: so runnes
> the water out
> finis.

A few quirks and inconsistencies: Keegan has provided illustrations to go with the entries for Lewis Carroll and Lear but not for Blake or Stevie Smith. The First and Second World War poets seem under-represented, with a single poem for Alun Lewis hardly enough. Among the few mistakes I noticed was a reference in the contents page to that well-known Northern Irish poet Derek Mayhew, presumably a hybrid of Derek Mahon and Sir Patrick Mayhew. Nor was it for the States, as Keegan claims in his preface, but for Paris that Pound left London in 1922. Dates for the poets would also have been helpful. And then there's the problem of the book's last stretch, which draws the line at anyone under fifty. It isn't just there the exclusions are felt: just as Sitwell and Spender looked forlorn and inadequate in the shadow of Hayward's cold-shouldered Celts, so too these pages suffer from our knowledge of the shifting centre of "English" poetry – shifting away from this book's definitions of "English" poetry, that is.

Reviewing Ricks's *Oxford Book of English Verse* for *Poetry Review* (Vol 89 No. 4, p.45), that fine poet and critic, the late William Scammell, lamented its smaller dimensions than Norton's *World Poetry*, and wondered whether the vast sprawl of English poetry could still be contained in a single volume. Maybe not, but in the meantime this may just have been the book he was looking for. In one of the volume's many enjoyable finds, George Farwell asks in a couplet of 1733: "Whether at Doomsday (tell, ye reverend wise) / My friend Priapus with myself shall rise?" Whatever you think about that, the reinvigorated canon that emerges from this marvellous book won't be lying down any time soon.

WENDY COPE

A best-seller from her first book, *Making Cocoa for Kingsley Amis* (Faber, 1986), Wendy Cope adheres more or less to the Larkin plan, which means that her first book since *Serious Concerns* (Faber, 1992) is only now about to appear: *If I Don't Know* (Faber, June). Relationship to the Zeitgeist and poetry-ideological allegiance are less relevant for her than for many of the poets in this issue: she is a classic English humorist, updated to take account of changing times. She honed her parodic skill on the poets who were the top guns in the 'eighties: Larkin, Hughes, Heaney, Raine, Hill, Causley, the Liverpools. She has yet to give us her New Generation parodies but we live in hope.

TIMEKEEPING

Late home for supper,
He mustn't seem drunk.
"The pob cluck", he begins,
And knows he is sunk.

STRESS

(for Henry Thompson, but not about him.)

He would refuse to put the refuse out.
The contents of the bin would start to smell.
How could she be content? That idle lout
Would drive the tamest woman to rebel.
And, now that she's a rebel, he frequents
The pub for frequent drink-ups with a mate
Who nods a lot whenever he presents
His present life at home as far from great.
The drinking makes his conduct even worse
And she conducts herself like some poor soul
In torment. She torments her friends with verse,
Her protest poems – dreadful, on the whole.
We daren't protest. Why risk an upset when
She's so upset already? I blame men.

SOPHIE HANNAH

All three of Sophie Hannah's books have been published since New Generation in 1994. Although she's not the kind of poet likely to feature in such a promotion, New Generation may have had an influence on her. For, although, as a female light-verse writer, she was instantly compared to Wendy Cope, as her work has developed it often looks closer to that of Glyn Maxwell. Whereas Cope always writes in a common-sense Larkinesque mode, Hannah likes grotesquerie, something that is always lurking behind English verse: the Lewis Carroll streak. Her subject matter is almost entirely concerned with her love life but for the reader the main interest lies in the backdrop to these affairs: an hilarious melange of lugubrious place names like Shugborough, seedy trains, multiple chain shops like the Edinburgh Woollen Mill, mini-cab drivers and ticket collectors. Her latest collection is *Leaving You and Leaving You* (Carcanet, 1999). She has also written two novels: *Gripless* (Arrow, 1999) and *Cordial and Corrosive* (Arrow, 2000).

DARK MECHANIC MILLS

A car is a machine. It's not organic.
It is a man-made thing that can be fixed,
Maybe by you, as you are a mechanic

Although I must admit that I have mixed
Feelings about your skills in this connection.
You shrug and say my engine sounds "right rough".
Shouldn't you, then, proceed with an inspection?
Looking like Magnus Mills is not enough.

Resemblance to a Booker Prize contender
Has a quaint charm but only goes so far.
When servicing formed the entire agenda,
When I had no real trouble with my car,
Our whole relationship was based upon it,
This likeness, but you can't go in a huff
If I suggest you open up the bonnet.
Looking like Magnus Mills is not enough.

I lay all my suggestions on the table:
Fuel pump or filter, alternator, clutch,
The coil or the accelerator cable,
Or just plain yearning for the oily touch
Of a soft rag in a mechanic's fingers.
That's not your style at all. You merely grin.
Is it your Booker confidence that lingers?
I don't know why. You didn't even win.

You laugh as if you can't see what the fuss is
When I explain my car keeps cutting out.
I know that Magnus Mills has driven buses;
That's not the way I choose to get about.
I'm sorry that it has to end so badly
But I am up to here with being towed
And I'd take a clone of Jeffrey Archer, gladly,
If he could make my car move down the road.

SIMON ARMITAGE

Armitage is the poet for whom New Generation's slogan 'Poetry is the new rock 'n roll' was coined. He has been immensely busy since '94, publishing three new collections, the travel book *Moon Country* (with Glyn Maxwell), the anthology, *The Penguin Book of British and Irish Poetry Since 1945* (with Robert Crawford), the prose narrative *All Points North* and a version of Euripides: *Mister Heracles* (reviewed on p.57). He has generally consolidated his reputation as the front man of his generation. Armitage is the most imaginative and prolific poet now writing: who else would have taken on the challenge of the Millennium poem, 1000 lines, even if it was at a rate of £5 a line? The result, *Killing Time*, is a bold retake on MacNeice's *Autumn Journal*, using the same stanza. His *Selected Poems*, due from Faber in September, will show just how many poems he's written that will last. His prose book *All Points North* demonstrated his sure touch with popular narrative and this year he joins the ranks of the poet-novelists with *Little Green Man*, published by Penguin in August.

CHAINSAW VERSUS THE PAMPAS GRASS

It seemed an unlikely match. All winter unplugged,
grinding its teeth in a plastic sleeve, the chainsaw swung
nose-down from a hook in the darkroom
under the hatch in the floor. When offered the can
it knocked back a quarter-pint of engine oil,
and juices ran from its joints and threads,
oozed across the guide-bar and the maker's name,
into the dry links.

From the summerhouse, still holding one last gulp
of last year's heat behind its double doors, and hung
with the weightless wreckage of wasps and flies,
moth-balled in spider's wool . . .
from there, I trailed the day-glo orange power-line
the length of the lawn and the garden path,
fed it out like powder from a keg, then walked
back to the socket and flicked the switch, then walked again and coupled
the saw to the flex – clipped them together.
Then dropped the safety catch, and gunned the trigger.

No gearing up or getting to speed, just an instant rage,
the rush of metal lashing out at air, connected to the main.
The chainsaw with its perfect disregard, its mood
to tangle with cloth, or jewellery, or hair.
The chainsaw with its bloody desire, its sweet tooth
for the flesh of the face and the bones underneath,
its grand plan to kick back against nail or knot
and rear up into the brain.
I let it flare, lifted it into the sun
and felt the hundred beats per second drumming in its heart,
and felt the drive-wheel gargle in its throat.

The pampas grass with its ludicrous feathers
and plumes. The pampas grass, taking the warmth and light
from cuttings and bulbs, sunning itself,
stealing the show with its footstools, cushions and tufts
and its twelve-foot spears.

This was the sledgehammer taken to crack the nut.
Probably all that was needed here was a good pull or shove,
or a pitchfork to lever it out at its base.
Overkill. I touched the blur of the blade
against the nearmost tip of a reed – it didn't exist.
I dabbed at a stalk that swooned, docked a couple of heads,
dismissed the top third of its canes with a sideways sweep
at shoulder height – this was a game.
I lifted the fringe of undergrowth, carved at the trunk –
plant-juice spat from the pipes and tubes
or dust flew out as I ripped into pockets of dark, secret warmth.

To clear a space to work,
I raked whatever was severed or felled or torn
towards the dead zone under the outhouse wall, to be fired.
Then cut and raked, cut and raked, till what was left
was a flat stump the size of a manhole cover or barrel lid
that wouldn't be dug with a spade or prized from the earth.
Wanting to finish things off, I took up the saw
and drove it vertically downwards into the upper roots,
but the blade became choked with soil or fouled with weeds,
or what was sliced or split somehow closed and mended behind,
like cutting at water or air with a knife.
I poured barbecue fluid into the patch

and threw in a match – it flamed for a minute, smoked
for a minute more, and went out. I left it at that.

In the weeks that came, new shoots like asparagus tips
sprang up from its nest, and by June
it was riding high in its saddle, wearing a new crown.
Corn in Egypt. I looked on
from the upstairs window like the midday moon.

Back below stairs on its hook, the chainsaw seethed.
I left it a year, to work through its man-made dreams,
count back across time
to what grass never knew to forget.
The seamless urge to persist was as far as it got.

If it ain't broke, don't fix it….

by Sheenagh Pugh

SIMON ARMITAGE
Mister Heracles
Faber, £7.99
ISBN 0 572 20333 7

THIS IS A re-working of the Euripidean play often known as *The Madness of Herakles*. Armitage says he wants "to re-present the play in the here and now, combining… eternal, universal issues with the undeniable changes that have taken place in the last two and a half thousand years".

I assume he feels it will then speak more immediately to a modern audience. For anyone unfamiliar with the most famously broken-backed play in history, in the first half, the wife, children and father of the absent hero Herakles are threatened with death by a cruel king, Lykos. At the last moment, Herakles returns, saves them and kills Lykos, to ecstatic approbation from the chorus. With Herakles offstage with his family, having movingly declared his love for them, the chorus reflects that "the gods still favour a just cause" (the Penguin Philip Vellacott translation, 1963).

Only they don't. Hera is still Herakles' enemy (purely because his mother was Zeus's mistress). She sends Iris and Madness to strike Herakles with a mania in which he kills his wife and children. When he comes round and contemplates his crime he sees no option but death. What saves him is human love, in the shape of his friend Theseus, who refuses to turn from him and leads him to a new life.

I have loved this play always, in various translations, but I never felt it needed help to speak to me. When Herakles hides his head, unable to look at his work or show his face, I don't need to think of him as "Mister Heracles" to feel for him, nor does his use of a bow rather than a gun distance him from me. And try comparing Euripides' ending, in Vellacott:

I, who have shamefully made destitute my house,
Will follow Theseus like a helpless wreck in tow.
If any man thinks wealth or power of greater worth
To him who has them, than a good friend – he is
mad

with Armitage's "rewritten":

Let him who brought down his whole house in shame
be drawn away, physically, to some place,
and occupy himself, not other minds.
Come down to earth, back to personal space.

The first speaks to me immediately while the second is woolly and baffling. It is also self-limiting in its use of the fashionable "personal space", which in five years may look very dated. Armitage hopes the version has "something of tomorrow" as well as today. There is no better way to ensure it does not than to fill it with topical idioms and references.

I don't want to be totally negative. At times Armitage's version is moving – e.g. when Herakles leads his wife and children into the house. Vellacott has:

Come then, and hold my hands.
I'll take these little ships in tow. I never find
Children a trouble. All men are the same at heart
Towards children

Armitage's is arguably more memorable:

Sail in my slipstream,
my candle afloat
and my paper boats.
Here is all mankind,
whole and unbroken,
a man and woman
born to their children.

It is puzzling that, having kept Euripides' image of the boat here, he does not also keep its savage echo at the end, when Herakles is led off "like a wreck in tow".

One central theme, guilt, survives almost intact. Herakles kills his family in a madness sent from outside and beyond his own control. Whether or not we believe "madness" comes from vengeful gods, it's arbitrary and unjust and, logically, carries no guilt. Nowadays, Herakles would be surrounded by the counselling industry telling him he wasn't to blame. But he knows better. Even if it came from outside, it was visited on a man capable, given that visitation, of killing his family as he had others – in the original, he knows even when mad that they are children but thinks them those of his enemy. The savagery that delights the chorus when he kills Lykos is the same quality he turns on his own. Nor

can he blame gods for his deeds – Armitage feels a need to kill off Zeus to point out that man is responsible for his own actions but Euripides' Herakles seems well aware of that. It is why he takes into exile the bow with which he killed his family. It's agony to hold, but is also who he is, what made him a hero and a murderer, and he knows he cannot escape it.

Armitage makes the bow a gun, but the debate Herakles has with himself about keeping it has gone, inexplicably. Gun or bow, it's still the potent symbol of what he is and has done, and in the introduction Armitage does talk of him "still carrying his weapons of murder". But the debate surely mattered as much as its conclusion.

Two more things I wish he hadn't fixed. First, in the debate between Iris and Madness, Armitage has Iris assign a reason for what will happen to Herakles: a suggestion that he has neglected the gods – "we were expecting him at our reception first". Even this trivial reason is too much. The most terrifying thing about Euripides is that there is no reason, no justification, for what gods, or chance, or fate, do; there doesn't need to be. (R. S. Thomas wouldn't have found that outdated.) Madness points out that Herakles has done nothing to deserve punishment. Iris replies, so what? "I only thought", says Madness, "how I might turn your path towards good" – and gets the chilling reply: "The Queen of Heaven did not send you here to think". Armitage's dialogue –

Madness: Peace talks – they're the way to sort problems out.

Iris: I'm sure some outpost with the Diplomatic
                                                    Corps
could be arranged. Now, if you don't mind?

– doesn't come near that for me. And I miss the stress on human friendship at the end. It is not absent from Armitage but in Euripides it is paramount. The world is arbitrary and unfair, our actions are shaped by things beyond our control (our past, malevolent others, chance) but they are still our responsibility, and only human friendship makes life bearable. It is Theseus' reaching out, the only redemptive factor, that makes the play bearable to read and I don't feel enough of it here.

SEAN O'BRIEN

No poetic reputation has firmed up more solidly than Sean O'Brien's since 1994. As if goaded by his exclusion from New Generation (he was just the wrong side of the age cut-off point), he seems to have been intent on fulfilling a hegemonic master plan. He published a critical book *The Deregulated Muse* and the anthology *The Firebox* in 1998. Together, these books established him as the poet-editor-critic of his generation. His poetry has gained in power, winning the Forward Prize for *Ghost Train* in 1995. His new collection, *Downriver*, is reviewed on p.61. In his piece in *Strong Words* he says: "Work, John Kinsella will do that for us". But, in fact, a list of O'Brien's own recent activities is dizzying; he has recently been writing plays: *Laughter When We're Dead* will be broadcast on R3 in June; *Downriver*, a jazz musical co-written with the composer Keith Morris, was premiered at the Newcastle Playhouse in February this year. He is now writing *Keepers of the Flame*, a verse play, set in the 1930s / 1990s, about fascists, poets and gunrunners and *Is that a Fact*, another verse play. Plus reviews for the *Sunday Times*, the *TLS* and the *Guardian*.

RIVER-DOORS

River-doors are not sea-doors. They open
Through mirrors and library shelves,
Through glasshouse sweat and damp attic walls.

They are the isomers of boredom.
Fleeing through a river-door the adult world's critique
You will hear the foul yawn of low tide caught

Au naturel in its khaki-tripe skin
Between the dented ironclad revetments
Of Drypool and Scott Street:

Barges, drowned dogs, drowned tarts, all are
Subdued to its element, worked
Into the khaki, with ropes and old staithes,

Estuarine polyps and leathery excrescences
No one has thought of a name for.
So much for childhood. Later you sit

From the long afternoon to the full moon's evening,
Blowing your dole on the landlord's voice:
At high tide, he says, in that intimate gurgling tone,

The river revisits his cellar,
Caressing the chains of the exciseman's ghost
Where he swings between this world and water's; but no,

It is never convenient to go down and see for yourself
How the river might stand at the foot of the steps.
The problem's the safety. The wife. It's the council,

He says, giving off the warm odour of bullshit.
However, you seem to be drinking the river in mild
And be eating its fruits from the pickled-egg jar

And as the product of refreshment hear
The river-door quietly open downstairs
Under the weight of the waters.

NOONDAY

The sultry back lane smells of fruit and shit
While everybody's binbags wait, stacked up
Like corpses in the ditch before Byzantium,
Late morning on the last day in the world.
The sun stands in the heavens. One by one
The black bags split asunder to disgorge
White regiments of maggots seething quietly.
At Rhodes, the Knights concealed the engineer
Who fashioned them the leather stethoscope
That diagnosed the *gazi* mining in the walls;
But gave the Sultan's nephew back to death –
And what is there in this to understand?

Great Suleyman, the one men call Magnificent,
Let it be night. Now let us hear the owl
Calling in the towers of Afrasiab,
The spider spin in ixarette around the Porte
The caravels go home to Venice burning
And in a velvet bag the severed head
Be brought for your inspection. No reply.
So later, from the noonday heat, we come
To beg the shade and silence of an hour
In Suleyman's branch library at Rhodes,
A cool white cage five paces cross, where nothing
Dares to live or rot without his word.

At the Helm

by Peter Porter

SEAN O'BRIEN

Downriver

Picador, £6.99
ISBN 0330 48195 9

IT'S PLEASANT TO be proved right. Twenty years or so ago I suggested that a new school of poetry was emerging which would take up the baton from Auden's Thirties Generation and bring back intellectualism and populism to British Poetry. I may have called its members by various vulgarisms, such as Provincial Dandies or North of England Surrealists, but I always knew who these poets were. Sean O'Brien, Peter Didsbury, Douglas Houston, Ian Duhig, Don Paterson in the van, with Michael Donaghy their special ancillary. Allied figures included W. N. Herbert, Glyn Maxwell and Simon Armitage. Already my line-up is in trouble, as there is nothing Northern about Glyn Maxwell. But I saw this grouping as delivering us from the Oxford Praetorians around Craig Raine and the hermetically sealed Old Experimenters in J. H. Prynne's Cambridge. The chief joy I expected from this new poetry was sheer interest: however technically accomplished the work – and its creators cared enormously about versification – it was the sharply observed and wittily presented material which counted. Their motto might have been Auden's "What do you think of England, this land of ours where no-one is well?" That question was asked as long ago as 1932. It is being asked again in potent terms in the new millennium.

My self-congratulation as a prophet is a churlish way of acknowledging the excellence of Sean O'Brien's new collection. *Downriver* is not just his strongest book to date, it is a consummate poetical performance, the announcement, as it were, of his having reached his perihelion. He writes with the ease and assurance of a poet so at home with the real world and its multiple surfaces that he can locate in each identifiable object, person or place a relevant symbol or portent. In earlier days O'Brien's poems sometimes tended to be strangled Laocoon-wise by their ramifications, their lineation and syntax tangling like roots in a pot. *Downriver* does not have one poem of this tortured order, which is especially admirable given that the tone of the book is that of an angry analyst, disgusted as much by spurious reforms (the New Labour tinta) as by vistas of social wreckage spread across the contemporary landscape.

O'Brien can seem like a Left-inclined Geoffrey Hill, a resemblance which would not endear itself to him. He celebrates the Versalian core of Britain almost in Hill's manner but calls up a different set of *dramatis personae* – the victims, the unpowerful, the put-upon, instead of Hill's warriors, churchmen and statesmen. Yet for him, as much as for Hill, the past is alive within the present and today's miseries and unfairnesses are endemically Albionic:

> Your hundred streets, your twenty names, all gone.
> A stink of burning sofas in the rain,
> Of pissed-on matresses, and poverty's
> Spilt milk, its tiny airless rooms designed
> To illustrate the nature of subjection
> To its subjects. They tell me politics
> And history are done: here's grease
> Extruded from the dripping tar-skinned walls
> Of workingmen's hotels; the ropes of hair
> Trapped in the sinks; the names perpetually denied
> A hearing, waiting in the smoky halls
> For their appointments with an age that bred
> And killed and then forgot them –
>
> ('Nineties')

The first part of *Downriver* pursues such historical detritus and its shriveled heritage savagely; 'Indian Summer', for instance, amounts to a newly-minted 'Field of Folk' "helmeted-airman" synopsis of a haunted and wounded world.

> If I am doomed to winter on the Campo Mediocrita
> Whose high plateau becomes the windy shore
> Of an ocean with only one side, to wait
> Where the howling sunshine does not warm me,
> Let us speak your tongue at least –
> For yours is the music the panther laments in,
> Retreating to Burradon, yours is the silvery
> Script of the spider at midnight,
> Your diary is scandal's pleasure-ground
> From which a bare instant of cleavage or leg
> Is all I shall have to sustain me.

The poem is written from within "the dark house (which) is a coffin of laws". It is a key work in the poet's rhetorical summary of present disquiet, an example of his tendency towards transcendence, to put a nimbus of mysticism around political philippic.

There is one quality in *Downriver* which marks it out from O'Brien's previous volumes. Though his move from Brighton back to the North of England of his upbringing happened several years ago, it is only now that a fresh and virtuosic liberation of language, achieved in markedly popular forms, has come to the fore in his writing. There is nothing in this approach of that lazy, too-often-encountered celebration of flinty Northern integrity contrasted with Southern complacency. Rather, it is a recovering of a vernacular which owes much to cabaret, song-writing, and political theatre, and incidentally to precursors of a decidedly Southern cast of mind. 'Song Books' (cycles and individual numbers) of various kinds occupy the second part of the collection. *The Drowned Book*, *The Black Path*, *Downriver* (a musical evocation of the Tyne and neighbouring commercial waterways), and *Sports Pages* are celebrated in varied lyrics, adding up to a veritable *Carmina Britannica* for our time. These are splendidly liberated and scurrilous inventions, eminently singable and shoutable. They belong to the same genre as O'Brien's recent verse play, *Laughter When We're Dead*, mounted in a small theatre in Newcastle last year, where parody and up-to-the-minute satire coalesce. *Laughter...* is a descendent of the Jacobean Revenge play, its idiom a mixture of Rory Bremner with claws, and Caryl Churchill able to scan. Rhyming couplets are never going to sound the same in pantomime. The Southern masters I named among O'Brien's influences are Gavin Ewart, Kit Wright and James Fenton, the latter in his vein of *Manila Envelope* and *The Empire of the Senseless*. Further off are such lyrics as 'Sing first that green remote Cockaigne' and 'At Dirty Dick's and Sloppy Joe's'. This collection of lampoons and ballads belongs to an as-yet-uncompiled set of 'Songs of Experience' which O'Brien and Ian Duhig appear to be composing for our improvement. Their natural exuberance appeals even more than their satiric analysis.

> Your mother keeps a rolling pin to warn off
> Me and other monsters of the billows
> But I recall my clothing was all torn off
> When last we laid our heads upon her pillows
> The likes of me sustain a great tradition
> We draw the straightest line across the sea
> So help me by assuming the position
> And opening your compasses to me.

O'Brien has yet another surprise to spring. He has hit on parody, and not such gentle parody either, as the latest of Versions of Pastoral.

'Ex Historia Geordisima' looks across the map of contemporary poetry and serves up a late night entertainment which should warn off Wannabees wherever they may be taking up their pens. As can happen when the parodist is a master, these are good poems in their own right. I forbear from naming their subjects but readers of today's verse will spot them easily. These same readers, however, should recognise what supreme skill lies beneath such professional jousting.

Poetry does not have a Register of Members' Interests, as Parliament does. But it behoves me to declare a few of mine. I am one quarter of the dedicatees of *Downriver* and it contains a poem written for my seventieth birthday. I used to assert that it is easier to review an enemy with magnanimity than a friend unfavourably. I should add that it is even harder to review a friend enthusiastically, since the world of letters will cheerfully detect bias. My bias in favour of O'Brien was established years ago. I am therefore particularly pleased that this book gives me no cause to modify my appreciation. Indeed, it does the opposite. O'Brien is writing better than ever.

> There is one quality in *Downriver* which marks it out from O'Brien's previous volumes. Though his move from Brighton back to the North of England of his upbringing happened several years ago, it is only now that a fresh and virtuosic liberation of language, achieved in markedly popular forms, has come to the fore in his writing. There is nothing in this approach of that lazy, too-often-encountered celebration of flinty Northern integrity contrasted with Southern complacency.

PAUL FARLEY

Paul Farley is the youngest member of what has become an influential school of recent British poets. Sean O'Brien is the senior figure and Farley's work first became known through his advocacy. Don Paterson is the intermediate figure in terms of age and all three are published by Picador, the list Paterson edits. Farley is at home in the micro-worlds of contemporary subcultures (his first collection, *The Boy from the Chemist is Here to See You*, Picador, 1998, was an essential book of the 'nineties according to the hip magazine *Select)* and he also has an archivist's love of the arcana of recently expired cultures: old vinyl records, films, even old paper sizes. Farley is the poet of a major shift in contemporary life: from things in themselves to their representation in media – media, that is, in the widest sense. He was *Poetry Review*'s Geoffrey Dearmer Poet of the Year in 1997. *The Boy from the Chemist* won the Forward First Collection Prize in 1998. He is currently Wordsworth Fellow at Grasmere; a new collection is due from Picador in February 2002.

BIG SAFE THEMES

You can look all you like but the big safe themes are there
all around, forestalling what you were going to say.
A robust description of a cedarwood cigar box
has grown so big it could now contain Cuba and history.

No refuge in things. They stand at one or two removes
from the big themes: so any warm weather fruit might bring
visiting times and the loved one we begged not to leave
as soon as you sniff at the rind or spit out a pip.

You can start with a washer, a throat pastille, a mouse mat
and watch them move in like the weather. Trying to be brave
ends in tears: I've seen the big safe themes walk all over
incest and morris dancing in their ten-league boots.

Why resist anyway? Bend with the big safe themes.
Let them do what they will and admit that the road you walk
again and again – right down to its screw-thread of blood
in a quivering phlegm – is becoming your big safe theme.

THE GLASSWORKS

I've taken to sitting on this side passing through here
because I'm falling in love with the glassworks. The driver
is smitten too: he slows down for this length of the track
and we open our minds to its mysteries: a yard in the back
where puddles are set in a slurry of gravel and silica,
the marine blues and greens of its chutes and bays, the exotica
these must lead into; its thousand degrees, its extrusions
and alchemy. And as usual the syrup-forms harden
into words for a moment, and though I can't speak for the driver,
flashing by, in no particular order,
come David Bowie squashed flat on the cover of *Lodger*;
the crack I made playing in Solon Street with my old caser;
the way Harry Worth found the right angle, bifurcated
himself, and, using his own reflection, levitated;
the glazier gag, an offshoot of the invisible rope trick,
dark origins of "daylight robbery" and rectangles of brick;
whatever it was/is between "the snow and the huge roses";
the lump of N5 that came crashing through in the small hours;
policemen's boots on the frame when we thought we'd been abandoned;
Lewis's, Boodles, T. J. Hughes' and Ethel Austin's;
the floor of tour boats and the clarity of the Aegean;
the roof of a grotto beneath a tench pond in a garden;
the slow molten myth of the thickness towards old sills;
betting my dole on the square, arched or round of Play School;
the Kitemarks of sea level that toughen at depths or heights:
the piece on my Airfix 1/25 *Spirit of St Louis* I couldn't fit;
sashes and port-holes and skylights and transoms and screens;
pebbled and wired and tinted, vessels or vitrines;
sharp for a moment then running like rain on a window,
like this one (I sigh like a lover) I'm looking through now.

MONIZA ALVI

Moniza Alvi had only published one collection at the time of New Generation. Her two collections since, *A Bowl of Warm Air* and *Carrying my Wife* (Bloodaxe, 2000), have established her uniquely playful voice: a blend of fantasy and gentle surrealism, often undercut by a dry irony ("These are strange people, he thought – / an Empire and all this washing, / the underwear, the Englishman's garden"). Critics have increasingly recognized her special qualities: Linda France said of *The Country at my Shoulder* – "Her imagination is always exotic and nimble, with the consistent and satisfying depth of an articulate emotional source". *Carrying My Wife* adds a new dimension in the title sequence in which she adopts the persona of a man: "And I envied her the baby within, / tried to cultivate my own – / ...a man impregnated with light and dark, / with violet, with the wrong food, / with small bottles of beer".

EINE KLEINE NACHTMUSIK

(After the painting by Dorothea Tanning)

You can lock the doors, even
bolt the air, but there's no way
of keeping your daughters in at night.
It doesn't matter how old they are –
three or four, six or seven –
a tornado throws them down the path
and ravishes them.
Stars glint like metal in their hair.
The darkness, fine as artists' ink,
seeps into their nightclothes.
If you follow them down the path –
you turn to stone.

Then long after the midnight hour
the wind flings them back into the hallway
and up onto the landing
with its cracked green paint.
Their blouses open up like curtains
on their narrow, childish chests.

Your daughters grow giant sunflowers
in the gloom.
Their hair streams upwards
thick as cypress trees.

ROGER McGOUGH

McGough's recent work has all the famous timing and wordplay intact but his subjects are often more sombre (though, not always, as the poem here shows). The title poem of his most recent collection, *The Way Things Are* (Penguin, 1999) uses a child's lop-sided innocence to high-light the facts of life: "No, old people do not walk slowly because they have plenty of time / Gardening books when buried will not flower. / Though lightly worn, a crown may leave a scar, / I am your father and this is the way things are". One of the most popular poets ever since his debut in the 'sixties, McGough's literary repuation, once assailed by the likes of Ian Hamilton, is more secure than ever. 'Let me die a young-man's death' was justly voted one of the Top Ten Nation's Favourite Poems in 1996.

MEETING THE POET AT VICTORIA STATION

A day off for you to recover from jetlag
and then the tour begins in Brighton.
Neither met nor talked, but I like your poems
and the face on the back of your Selected.

No sign of you under the station clock
nor at the ticket-office, so I make my way
to platform 12. Do I hear castanets?
Tap-dancers busking for the pure fun of it?

No. Sitting on the floor, back to the wall
surrounded by bags, books and foolscap,
a woman is pounding a typewriter, oblivious
of commuters stepping around and over her.

You are dressed all in black, wearing glasses,
and your hair is wilder than in the photograph.
Not too late for me to turn back and ring
the Arts Council: "Laryngitis"… "Gingivitis"… " St. Vitus"

Instead, I ask you to dance. You give me your hand
and I whisk you across the marble floor,
my arm around your waist in the old-fashioned way.
Waltz, Foxtrot, Villanelle, Quickstep.

Ticket Inspectors clear the way for us
as I guide you in and out of Knickerbox.
Shoppers stop and applaud as we twirl
around the shelves of W. H. Smith and Boots.

A Tango so erotic that Victoria blushes.
Rush hour but nobody is going anywhere
except in a centipedic circle as we lead
the customers in a Conga round the concourse.

A voice over the tannoy: "Take your partners..."
Rumba, Samba, Salsa, Sestina.
Things are hotting up as the tempo quickens
Charleston, Terza Rima, Cha Cha Cha.

Suddenly the music stops.
"Excuse me" I say, "Are you the poet?"
Removing her glasses she looks up from the typewriter.
"How did you guess?" I help carry her bags to the train.

ANNE STEVENSON

Anne Stevenson's *Granny Scarecrow* (Bloodaxe, 2000), which was short-listed for the Eliot and Whitbread prizes, marked a welcome return after a period of poetic silence. Jem Poster said of the book; " Stevenson reaches back into a past already pregnant with a future now known to her, traversing family history with an ease which might be described as playful if her disclosures were not so chilling". Anne Stevenson's poetry is characterised by its intellectual rigour, its searching emotional candour, and its alertness to the oddities of experience. *Granny Scarecrow* is remarkable for its balance of philosophical enquiry, sharp observation and (despite age, loss and deafness) high spirits. T. S. Eliot took a famously jaundiced view of "the gifts reserved for age"; Stevenson is more affirmative: "Consciousness walks on tiptoe through what happens. / So much is felt, so little of it said. / But ours is the breath on which the past depends. / What happened is what the living teach the dead".

CASHPOINT CHARLIE

My office, my crouch, is by the Piccadilly cashpoint where
Clients of the Hong Kong and Shanghai Banking Co.
Facilitate my study of legs as they ebb and flow;
Legs, and the influence of sex and wealth on footware.

The human foot – wedge-shaped, a mini torso –
Used to be, like the monkey's, toed for zipping
Fast through jungles. Just how prehensile gripping
Got to be a closed shop for hands I'll never know.

Anyhow, feet are in jail now, shoes' prisoners,
Inviting comparison, ladies, with steel-tipped bullets,
And sadly, gentleman, with coffins. My tiptop favourites
Are Dr. Martin's hammer-like hoofs and laceless trainers.

It's a proved fact that the shabbily shod give more.
Like knee-slashed jeans give more than knife-creased trousers.
And shivering junkies more than antique browsers.
What? Thanks to a glitch in the chem lab (not a war)

I'm legless. Or as good as... it all depends
On where you poke and what you count as me.
To "rise" I use a crutch. It helps the money,
And, like my filthy sleeping bag, offends

Your everyday dainty British git just bad enough
To make him pull his Balaclava face
Hard down over his sweet guilt. I make my case:
OK, if you hate me, you have to hate yourself,

And think it steady at him. Nothing's said, of course.
They never meet your eyes, not even the women
Yanking at their big-eyed kids like I was poison,
And then, with a tight look, opening their purse.

It's crazy, but I love them... it... taking the piss.
If that old guy, that Greek philosopher in his barrel,
Could see me now, in my sleeping bag, beside a hole
In a wall that spits out money, he'd be envious.

GRACE NICHOLS

Grace Nichols' poetry is imbued with Caribbean warmth and *joie de vivre*, often making a contrast with British uptightness and reserve. Her poem 'Skanking Englishman Between Trains' is characteristic: "he was alive / was full-o-jive / said he had a lovely / Jamaican wife". Her latest collection, *Sunris* (Virago, 1996), celebrates carnival in the long title poem. This is a wide-ranging poem which brings out the mythic and elemental aspects of carnival, makes links to Africa and the Aztec kingdoms, and pulses with the sounds and colours of the spectacle. Deeply Caribbean in sensibility, she writes sensitively of other traditions, especially Africa and India. Her reaction to the hurricane of 1987 ('Hurricane Hits England') is interesting: hurricanes are Caribbean not English, so its appearance here is welcomed: "Ah sweet mystery / Come to break the frozen lake in me". Recently she has written much for children: a new adult collection is needed.

Gillian Cargill

ECLIPSE

For such audacity, the ancients
would have predicted
a litter of floods
across the face of earth –
an omen from
the leaf of life
a warning from
the book of years.

To mark the significance for us;
the cat disappeared upstairs,
the dog next door stopped
its incessant howling,
even the grass listened
to the silence,
the small primeval coolness
that reigned for two minutes.

And in the eerie half-glow
between the depleted sun
and the moon's great shadow,
we got a glimpse,
an evolutionary flashback –
past dinosaur, past genesis,
an inkling of the first-dark,
the black amnesia of the beginning.

JACKIE KAY

Jackie Kay first came to notice with *The Adoption Papers* (Bloodaxe, 1991), a brave and spirited look at the adoption process, from all sides, done in different voices and typefaces. Her work has great brio. Bessie Smith is one of her heroines and she has written a prose book about her and a verse play, in which Smith's indomitable spirit is celebrated. Her fascination for jazz has also produced a highly successful novel, *Trumpet* (Picador, 1999) which won the *Guardian* Fiction Prize. Her latest collection, *Off Colour* (Bloodaxe, 1998), was shortlisted for the T.S. Eliot Prize. The poems in *Off Colour* deal with sickness, both of the individual and society. At times the poems are Plathian in their tormented writhings: "My blood sugar is soaring. My tongue is so sugary / I flatter my enemies. My healthy booming enemies. / I say sweet things when I want to weep and spit". A collection of short stories, *Trout Friday*, will be published by Picador next year.

HOP PICKERS RETURNING 1883

(After a painting by Alexander Mann)

When she returns home across the long green field
The early moon is behind her, tight as her bun.
The thin light streaks and suffuses the earth, and the sky
Is as pink as her dusty cheeks.

Though tired, her body is light with grace.
Her fine hands mirror the bone colour moon.
Her dress is the same pink as her face, as the earth and the sky.
So that when she returns, walking the dirt dust track back,

By the tall grasses with her hat in her hand,
Past sheep – the colour of her apron and the moon –
She is returning home from the earth and the sky.
The hops, held in hopeful hands, and the light walk back

Is so familiar she seems in a floating trance.
She could be thinking or not, or sad, or not.
Perhaps she expected the rain to fall, from the sky to the earth
– For she carries a big black umbrella, like a raven

That has never flown, at her side – and it did not rain.
Or perhaps she has fallen out of love or love never came.
The light gently, slowly, sinks from the sky to the earth
As she sinks, walking home, under the fading light, calm.

When she looks out on the land from her window,
It will be pitch dark. It will be hard to fathom.
She will climb the stairs from the earth to the dark sky
To sleep the sleep that waits for the land to wake.

MAURA DOOLEY

David Hunter

Maura Dooley's work as an editor and programmer has sometimes diverted attention from her poetry. Jon Cook, in a review in *The Independent on Sunday,* perceptively noted that: "Her poems are themselves acts of displacement, turning around some event or emotion that cannot be fully named or known...an imagination which proliferates mysteries". This mode is an alternative to the variations boys play on tricks - learnt - from - Muldoon and has been influential with other women poets, such as Helen Dunmore, Kate Clanchy, and Colette Bryce. *Kissing a Bone* was published by Bloodaxe in 1996. Her latest book, *The Honey Gatherers* (due from Bloodaxe) is an anthology of love poetry. She is convenor of the new MA in Creative and Life Writing at Goldsmiths College, London.

ZOOLOGY

At seventeen the girls get the canteen
and the boys the elephant house.

Our atlases are cheap hotelware on which
the bloodied shores of India or Africa

spring from congealed beans. We swill and stack.
Under trees, Paul scrubs the rough grey flanks

of docile beasts, tenderly lifts ears like barn doors
and through the steam Anne and I can just see

Rosie trumpet like an angel, water spilling off
in great glorious showers. Guaranteed Unbreakable,

we swill and stack heavy white plates,
dreamy with the new world we know is ours.

An endangered species howls. The elephant, the boy,
the girls, the day, gather in their summer hours.

HELEN DUNMORE

Helen Dunmore is one of the few contemporary writers equally at home in poetry and fiction. Since her debut novel, *Zennor in Darkness* (Viking, 1993) she has sold over 300,000 books. Bill Turner identified her special quality as a poet: "She seems able to poach subliminal forebodings at will, resisting any rhetorical roll of drums to presage them, and suddenly we are in that hallucinatory other world. Sharing her viewpoint". Many of her poems are about nebulous moods, things which can't and won't last but she is sometimes powerfully direct, as in her Gulf War poems: "That killed head straining through the windscreen / with its rill of bubbles in the eye-sockets / is not trying to tell you something – // it is telling you something. / Do not look away, //...for God is counting / all of us who are silent / holding our newspapers up, hiding" ('Poem on the obliteration of 100,000 Iraqi soldiers'). Her new novel, *The Siege*, is published by Viking in June. A new *Selected Poems* is due from Bloodaxe.

THE MAN ON THE ROOF

When my grandmother died my father eulogised her.
There she was, coming home with the pram
and her crowd of children
when something strange in the light
or its impediment getting at her from heaven
made her look up to see one of her children –
her eldest child, her son, him –

upon the roof, riding the horse of the homestead
with wild heels, daring her to defy him
and get him down. She got him down
with a word, as he remembers it,
her lovely penny-pale face looking up at his
from the path where her children swarmed and shouted
and it was this

he remembered when her coffin lay under his hand:
the roof, and his coming down.

When our priest died I remembered him
up on the roof, mending a tile
– a little job on hand, and a hammer
and air of busyness to keep him busy
while he pretended not to be pretending
to ride the roof in its wild beauty

over the unfamilied air of Liscannor
and half-way to America. Maybe.
Or maybe merely tapping the tile in
like a good workman.
"How beautiful it was up on the roof"
he said to the people at Mass.

My father touched his mother's coffin
and did not say how golden her hair was.
Even I remember how golden it was
when the grey knot was undone.

Now they are gone into the ground,
both of them. They are riding on the roof,
their wild heels daring us to defy them,
and we are here on the ground
penny-pale and gaping.
They will not tell
how beautiful it is. I will not ask them.

VIRGIN WITH TWO CARDIGANS

There's a stone set in the car-park wall
down at knee-level
which commends her.

There is her stone, set in the car-park wall
its flinty lettering so bright-cut
it would blind her.

There are these relics: a scrap of wool,
a lost button, an unfollowed pattern.

Here, on this path, slowly, leaning
on two sticks, she still comes.
Trying to know all these new faces
she looks about her, tortoise-patient.

How patiently she wants God to unbutton
her two cardigans
but he is stubborn.

Here, buttoning her cardigans

with lumpy fingers she bungles
in the lee of the breeze-block wall,

Virgin with Pineapple
Virgin with the Globe as a Golden Ball

Virgin with Two Cardigans
pushing a pearl button
into the gnarl of its hole.

BENJAMIN ZEPHANIAH

Benjamin Zephaniah's facility with rap and ballad forms has made him one of the most popular poets in the county and his assured performances have made him a TV favourite. His two Bloodaxe collections, *City Psalms* (1992) and *Propa Propaganda* (1996) have established his reputation on the page. He ranges easily over domestic and international concerns: "We have Big Bombs / You have little bombs / You should sign a dotted line / Saying your bombs will stay small". In 1999, in an inspired Poetry Placement by the Poetry Society, he spent six months in the chambers of Michael Mansfield QC soon after the Steven Lawrence enquiry had reported. Zephaniah was fascinated and appalled by the way that legal language cuts across our natural ideas of justice, and the poems he wrote then, including the one here, reflect this.

BREAKFAST IN EAST TIMOR

Ana Pereira is chewing bloodstained oats
in a home-made home in East Timor.
This morning she woke up to a shower
Of bloodstained rain and the smell of common death.
She prayed uncontrollably to a European version of Jesus
Christ, then she went to visit her sister's grave.

She visits her sister's grave every day.

As she was returning home she purchased
An Indonesian newspaper, conceived and printed
in Jakarta. Now at her breakfast table
She is trying to understand why her occupiers

Are so interested in the British royal family,
The politics of the European community
And the peace talks in Northern Ireland.
She just can't understand why the British royal family
Are not interested in the grave of her sister
Or why Europe is so concerned with money.
She wonders what makes new British Labour so proud
Of its women and a thing called an ethical foreign policy.

Ana Pereira has the hands of a man,
Her ears can recognise the sound
Of a loaded Hawk fighter plane as she sleeps
And her feet are designed to dodge bullets.
You can see her killers in her eyes
And an ever present vigilance in her step.
She has carried all her sisters' coffins
On her reinforced shoulders,
She waved all her brothers goodbye
When they graduated to the rank of militants
And her distinguished stubbornness envies them,
She too wants to be in the hills.

She wants to know where her father is,
She hates bloodstained oats,
And she would love to visit Europe
To see for herself.
For now she will keep remembering,
Negotiating days
Leaving nothing to chance,
Nothing for the Indonesians
And nothing for nothing.

Today's breakfast tastes like yesterday's
And today, the death business continues.
Tomorrow she wants so much to be alive.

ELIZABETH BARTLETT

Adam Thorpe has called Elizabeth Bartlett "a kind of weird cross between Anne Sexton and Philip Larkin". This isn't as odd as it seems. Her poems range about a Larkin-like territory of desolate provincial scenes, but also have a raw confessional streak (so, come to think of it did Larkin's: "Love again, wanking at half past three" – perhaps he too was a weird cross between himself and Anne Sexton). But Larkin never wrote poems like 'With My Body': "I never knew this curious way before. / I was always taken flat on my back". Some of her poems, such as 'Design' do have a Larkin-like plangency ("The blanched eyes of the aspens / Quiver at the field's edge, their mad cascades / Of butterflies turn swift and brittle"); others, from her social work casebook, are closer to Peter Reading country: "He lay on the floor covered in shit, / as he had done all night on his fitted carpet" ('999 Call'). In the end, she is best treasured as a complete original – more of a Stevie Smith. Her New and Selected Poems, *Two Women Dancing* was published by Bloodaxe in 1995.

YAKHAL INKOMO*

She is like the judas goat in a slaughter house.
Build a wall between North and South, she says.
We do not know what to say.
Put them on the banana boats and send them back.

With her cut-glass voice and painted mouth
she tells us that she bought her ticket today
to visit China. The books that she got
for the course she reads diligently,
but she doesn't want to save the whale
or save the world. The badges we wear
offend, but every corner of the world
she goes to, swallows her money. We fail,
as they do, to enter the righteous and rare
country of her closed mind. Her tips
to solve the problems of religion and race
make her a lifelong exile, as her lips
form the words: *They are not like us.*

Displaying her designer clothes she sits
with her charm and grace against the wall
in the pride of her white women's dream,
watching the black bodies topple and fall.
She is a no-go area, she has a pass;

in her Sixth district there is no grass.
Inside her self-made prison she is free to go.
She doesn't hear the yakhal inkomo.

Yakhal inkomo – cry of cattle at the slaughterhouse.

Not By Scrag-End Alone

by Gillian Allnutt

ELIZABETH BARTLETT

Appetites of Love

Bloodaxe, £7.95
ISBN 1 85224 548 4

CATS HOLD THEIR own in the world of English poetry and Pushkin, with "his stilted walk, his slight fawn body, / and his blue eyes staring from that strange / dark mask, those affected brown suede boots", is no exception. He gets his come-uppance in death, though, from those who "wandered by ... / with cobby peasant heads and legs, / padding across the mounded turf, / and urinated daily where he lay". That's all right then. God's in his heaven.

And the good gardener's in the hot-house with his orchids: "he pulls the shades / for their testicular profiles, /adjusts the inner temperature, / scrutinises their fleshy phallic stems, / waters tuberous roots". Meanwhile: "Out in the real weather / the luteous sunflower nods and dips / like a giggling schoolgirl, / her big round head disturbs him" ('Sunflower'). It seems she's got what it takes, though: he ends up with his arms around her.

Out here with the cobby-coated cats and the luteous (deep orange-yellow, I looked it up) sunflower, there's a robustness to life – it's tough but we know how to handle it. And here are 'The Winter Gardens' of Elizabeth Bartlett's childhood: "A fabulous world, / we thought, hurrying to buy scrag-end, / our home-mended shoes stuttering unevenly, /making a different kind of music, / the long saga of being on the outside / looking in, beginning".

It's hard to survive on scrag-end alone, though, and sometimes the sassiness is stretched to the edge of savagery. The subject of 'A Caring Community' is a man with motor neurone disease who spends his time painting flowers at the day centre. "He is manic depressive too, / wouldn't you know?" And then he may have arthritis as well: "Cheer up, / they say, prodding him mercilessly. / He paints another flower / like a violent crucifix".

Not even savagery is left to salvage the world of "Gwennie, unmarried factory girl / of this estate, council house reared", whose veins will not admit entry to the "shunt" (plastic tube) of the dialysis machine: "she rejected / although not meaning to, their care / and would have to die instead". The dice are so loaded against Gwennie that only her death can redeem the situation – and perhaps not for herself so much as for the technicians, "all helpful men" who, however, "devoutly wished amen / when Gwennie ... / silently cried because her hair / grew lank and lost its curl" ('Dialysis').

These and other poems in the collection must be in part the fruits of Bartlett's working for many years in the Health Service. This is not the only institution that comes in for harsh treatment. Marriage and adult education get a rough ride too, though the latter is lightly handled in such poems as 'Music Appreciation' and 'Adult Education Happy Endings'.

Elizabeth Bartlett inhabits the bleak world of post-war, post-imperial and post-'God Is Dead – Nietzsche' Britain. It takes more than the scrag-end of courage to do that; and it takes more than her roving humour, often mordant, sometimes "just touching the edges of fantasy". It takes the kind of honesty expressed in 'Emmanuel Man', written for Richard, whose disease is "creeping into every organ" and whose paintings are "brilliant with colour and life". She wheels him out in his chair: "Careering through the park / I nearly tip you into the shrubs. / Halted, you scrutinise the bark. / 'That's like me. / It doesn't know whether to live or die.' / We laugh inordinately".

JOHN BURNSIDE

John Burnside's three collections since New Generation Poets – *Swimming in the Flood* (1995), *A Normal Skin* (1997), and *The Asylum Dance* (2000) (all Cape) – have dispelled any notion that he was the token nature poet in the group. Eschewing the English empirical tradition, taking bearings from Spanish poetry, and being unafraid of focussing on a metaphysical reality, Burnside's work has been compared to Geoffrey Hill's. Like many prolific poets, he has a characteristic *leitmotif* poem, which appears in different guises throughout his work: in the poems he is driving, in the late afternoon, the day is winding down, there are "tractors spilling hay", the land is "immense and bright, like memory", "the houses here are floating in the last / glimmer of the day". *The Asylum Dance* won this year's Whitbread Poetry Award.

THE ELECTRON MICROSCOPE

Because I could walk for hours
with a marmalade jar

and the long-handled net
I found in my grandfather's shed,

searching for the blue and crimson fish
from Rupert books, and the National Geographic,

I missed the lives that blend into the sand,
or vanish under ultraviolet,

the way I missed the heartbeat in a clam,
or overlooked the broth of fallen moss

and starling bones that gathered in an upturned
row boat at the foot of Mason's Yard.

One school of thought would have it that,
of all we kill from clumsiness or greed, it's not

the major animals that we'll regret
– orang utan, Miss Waldron's Colobus –

but something minuscule, or nondescript
that no one thought about, or even saw;

and how shall we keep
from missing it altogether, when we sit

all night beneath these strip-lights, making out
the fabric of the world, the twists and turns,

the curlicues and mazework, wisps of light
and gravity, in tiny, nameless scales.

Submerged Beauty

by Ian Tromp

JOHN BURNSIDE

The Asylum Dance

Jonathan Cape, £8.00
ISBN 0 224 05938 6

Angels and Animals

Maquette, £5,00
ISBN 1 902342-00 3

NOT FULLY UNDERSTANDING why, I knew I wanted to use the word "shimmer" to describe the poems in John Burnside's recent book and pamphlet. The word seemed to touch something in the poems that I couldn't quite express; something of the tangle of darkness and light that plays through them. Think of how, through water, a wreck or treasure might dance between seeing and disappearance. And then I discovered that "shimmer" derives from Norse and German words meaning, respectively and paradoxically, brightness and darkening. Both words – and their opposition – do well to evoke the disconcerting air of Burnside's poems, for there is here a current of disquiet. Within or beneath the apparent serenity of his gentle, questing voice there runs

a thread of darkness, an unsettled edge, which gives the poems a mix of lucid confidence and uncertainty, a sense of unease beneath their precise and wandering surfaces.

The pamphlet's title names the polarity of angelic and animal life that works through both publications. In a statement in *Strong Words: Modern Poets on Modern Poetry* (Bloodaxe, 2000), Burnside described poetry as a form of alchemy, therefore a means of change, a discipline of transformation. Specifically, he spoke of it as articulating the process of what he calls *living as a spirit* – "an *inventio*, by which we create ourselves from moment to moment, just as the world around us creates itself out of nothing". He intends here the cultivation of self-awareness rather than physical being, of spirit rather than body, the angelic and not the animal. So there is this aspect of a search in Burnside's poems, of poetry used as a philosophical or spiritual exercise.

But there remains a quiet unease within these books, which is not quite accounted for by the polarity of body and spirit, the disjuncture of angelic and animal. Rooted in the physical, several poems speak of meeting the world in and as a body: there is the concern in 'Geese' with "how the flesh belongs", or the descriptions in 'Sense Data' of "an earth-tide in the spine" and "music I could feel // like motion in the marrow of my bones", or, in 'Fields', the evocation of memory "somewhere in the flesh".

The undercurrent in Burnside's poems is no

Gnostic dualism. His philosophy includes the body, indeed begins within it, and circles around the question of what it is to be a spirit in a body. The body, after all, is our primal home, and it is to questions of home that *The Asylum Dance*, in particular, returns. In 'Settlements', Burnside speaks of "the notion of home: / not something held / or given / but the painful gravity / that comes from being settled on the earth". In 'Roads', he writes: "forgive me / being not the man I seem / not lost or found / but somewhere between". There is a lovely haiku by Basho:

> Hearing the cuckoo
> even in Kyoto
> I long for Kyoto

Perhaps this evokes what I'm trying to touch in writing of Burnside's poems: this odd, familiar, sensation of being not lost or found; being here, home, within the body, within the world, yet yearning for the present.

Burnside often writes with trailing lines that step across the page. A passage describing the sea off Anstruther speaks of "the sway of the tide" – this is how his lines move, swaying between the margins. Lineation is based more on breath and rhythm than on metre or rhyme, though some internal rhyme keeps fluidity in the lines. Sometimes this schema makes sense and is delightful – as when the section breaks mid-sentence in 'After Lucretius': "[...] when he disappears, / amidst the thaw / there is nothing to show he is missing, / not even // an absence"; sometimes it feels superfluous and arbitrary. In a few instances, lines read as sliced, unfurling prose, as in 'The Hay Devil':

> Where logic seems apparent:
> in bullfrogs
>   or Black-Eyed Susans
> bird migrations
>   patterns on the skin
> of newt or carp

This passage also demonstrates a difficulty I have with Burnside's poems, a quality that might again be encapsulated by referring to that word "shimmer". Jewel-like, his poems are compact and lustrous, but sometimes their flaring feels a little empty, their depth more apparent than real. This has more to do with diction than with content or phrasing. Sometimes the language – so figured and

weighty in its symbolism, so obviously meaningful – is just *too* pretty and tends to the precious. The repeated naming of herbs and spices is another instance of this: no doubt it is intended to root the verse in felt, sensed experience, but it can feel mannered.

That said, the poetry of these two volumes has seriousness and depth, a wondering philosophical air rendered with intimacy and an ear for evocative, limpid phrasing. In 'Ports', the opening poem of *The Asylum Dance*, Burnside speaks of

> the beauty of wreckage
>   the beauty
> of things submerged

This does well to describe my response to the poems. There is a sense of fragility and even fracture within them, a shimmer of doubt that is attractive and eroding, beautiful and ravaged.

PETER READING

Peter Reading (born 1946) was outside the New Generation frame, but then he's outside every frame. For some time his books – a body of work which tended to write off *Homo sap.* – seemed on the verge of self-termination. 1999's book was *Ob*, but that was quickly followed by *Marfan* and *Untitled*. Significantly Reading's latest poems give free rein to his ornithological bent, *Homo sap.* presumably having finally been despaired of. Reading the natural historian and Reading the classicist have always played second fiddle to Reading the Laureate of grot but this new phase is interesting. Reading wrote about tabloid atrocities (he didn't make them up you know) because he was a thwarted celebrant of the natural world, fine wines and the serene beauty of classical Greece (not that that didn't have its grot too).

EDUCATIVE

One day, when I was ten or thereabouts,
the Natural Science teacher, Mrs Hope,
assisted by the *Bug-Eye*, as we fondly
dubbed *Caliban* the Caretaker, turned up
trundling an ancient epidiascope
which she proceeded to plug in, adjust,
and focus until a rectangle of light
was dimly projected on the classroom wall.
Within the bright glow of the apparatus
she conjured a large illustrated book
until an image, furry, indistinct,
became apparent on the impromptu screen.

Children, these are serious times indeed . . .

It had been, once, a coney, but was now
a distorted, swollen, slimy face with eyes
bulging and blind (not *that* dissimilar
to those of the hapless Janitor).

                              Years on,
the distemper reached an island off the coast
of North Wales where I helped to break the backs
and pitch the bodies of the unfortunate,
infected creatures over the East Face cliff . . .
(We are all members of the Wildlife Trust.)

Forty more years, a Trustee is defining
Myxomatosis: *Viral disease in rabbits;*

produces fever; lesions of the skin
resembling myxomas; muscoid swelling
of mucous membranes; it exists in nature
in South American species of the genus
Sylvilagus, *and has been introduced*
to parts of Europe and Australia
as a means of rabbit population control . . .

Ladies and Gentlemen, back in '54,
an article in The Times *of July 1st*
reports that: "Myxomatosis, this past year,
has extirpated 90 per cent of burrows
in southern England alone. Farmers insist
that this is a virus vital in the control
of rabbits, which do vast amounts of damage –
some £50 million each year. However,
scientists warn that if you disturb the balance . . ."

[Somehow it seems a long way back to me:
the swollen, mucoid features, bulging, blind;
the conjured image, furry, indistinct;
the dim, projected concept in poor light;
the corrupt corpses of the unfortunate
(we are all members of the Wildlife Trust)
viewed through an ancient epidiascope;
the deluded ramblings of Old Ma Hope.]

THAT FIND OF LONGISQUAMA INSIGNIS,

oldest known feathered fossil evidence,
from a reptillian creature which most likely
glided between the trees in forest swamps
75 million years pre-*Archaeopterix*
in Central Asia, anticipated birds.

It had a furcula virtually the same
as modern birds, and *wasn't* a dinosaur.

What was the initial function of those feathers
(whose evolution probably antedates
the dinosaur)? Did they develop from scales
for insulation when warm blood arrived?

Or did these nascent plumes burgeon from ridges
along the back, and muscles then develop
in forelimbs, coincident with plumage growth,
enabling first flight?...

Sunt aliquid manes.

Cheerfulness breaking in

by John Whitworth

PETER READING

Marfan

Bloodaxe, £6.95
ISBN 1 85224 516 6

[untitled]

Bloodaxe, £7.95
ISBN 1 85224 563 0

ISABEL MARTIN

Reading Peter Reading

Bloodaxe, £10.95
ISBN 1 85224 467 4

I HAVE TALKED of and chewed over Peter Reading (the person, the phenomenon, the artefact) twice before in these pages. In 1987 I approved, and in 1989 I disapproved, rather po-facedly it now appears to me – at least that is the gist of an entry and a note in Isabel Martin's exhaustive, and occasionally exhausting *Reading Peter Reading*. Doubtless it is as she says, and when I get up to the loft again I can check it out. Why should Reading care anyway? What can Whitworth, the Light Verse acrobat, the Light Verse hard man (says Paul Hyland in *Getting into Poetry*) say of the Dark Verse much-harder-man Reading anyway? It's like asking Paul Merton about Kierkegaard.

Ah, but I have actually read Reading – not all of him, it is true, but a good chunk. And I go on reading Reading; there are unforgettable fragments, none more than this, quoted by Martin from 'Exegetic', which you probably know already:

This is unclean: to eat turbots on Tuesdays,
tying the turban unclockwise at cockcrow,
cutting the beard in a south-facing mirror,
wearing the mitre while sipping the Bovril,
chawing the pig and the hen and the ox-tail.

Further fatwa fodder follows, for Reading is a stout-hearted God-hater – a stout-hearted man-woman-and-child-hater too; not a hater of absolutely *everybody*, it's true, but he certainly didn't care for the redneck Marfans of Marfa, a small Texan town where he spent "a sinecure year" in 1995. And they don't sound nice:

The stupid guns of off-duty Patrolmen
At Carmens stuffing their porcine guts with shite
Before resuming the cat-and-mouse charade
Of rounding up the smooth-faced, terrified *hijos*

Those of us who want to, we all recognise Reading's godless Lucretian universe by now:

In unmarked graves and splendid catafalques
alike, impartial atoms metamorphose

A good Reading word "catafalque", good enough for him to recycle (recycling is part of his art). There is an Elizabethan largesse in his linguistic choices and Reading himself is a bit of an Elizabethan. Or perhaps, given his subject matter, a Jacobean, much possessed by death, and wickedness, and how the atomic arrangements that make up human beings are eternally disappointing. "I don't make it up, you know" he says, and though the "found" poems that swell out his *oeuvre* often turn out not to be found at all but composed (not that Reading ever said otherwise), I believe him. For sure he doesn't make it up: "Bledsoe & Swearingem [I swear it], Lawyers". You need an eye for it: I have come across Wake & Paine, the Funeral Directors of Twickenham, Lampon, the electrician of Colchester and Dr Kill the abortionist.

Meanwhile, back in Marfa, Juanita, grieving for her son, sees the Virgin and child baked into a tortilla:

> I saw the donkey. I saw the ears and head,
> And then the legs, and then I saw the Virgin
> Mary riding, holding the baby Jesus!

Reading prints a photocopy of the "epiphanic" tortilla in case we should doubt his word, but I wouldn't dream of doing so. To Larkin all the world is Larkinesque and Reading reads his runes honestly enough – they are there for all to see, but of course he sees them that little bit more easily

Isabel Martin, whose "pioneering" (meaning, I suppose, that Reading hasn't been done before) doctoral dissertation this is, translated from the German and "drastically" shortened (my God!) marches briskly and informatively from book to book, more than twenty books in all, and that doesn't count *[untitled]* which I have in front of me. This shelf-full was a part of Reading's strategy for success: "I knew when I started that if I wanted to get anywhere – not knowing anybody in the business – I had to bombard them with books". He did and it worked. As I remarked in print *vis-à-vis* Wendy Cope some years ago – Larkinian, Borgesian paucity is out. We're back to new Victorian chaps, ample chaps, Les Murray the Christian and Peter Reading the Atheist I'm thinking of particularly; the poets who not only talk a lot, they write one hell of a lot too and I think I'm all for that. Write the stuff, publish it if you can and let posterity winnow wheat from chaff. If poetry is what you do – then do it, for God's sake.

Reading does it, and though Martin divides the *oeuvre* into Early, Middle and Late period, I don't know that I do:

> "Just now all is stock dies – that Foot an Mouth year
>   afore last –
> An they says as e got debts an that's why e shot
>   isself".

That is early and this is late:

> A fellow lone Star drinker in Ray's Bar:
> "Whan ya git old ya can't remember a fuck".

Chips off much the same block, wouldn't you say? I'm not complaining. A lot of the stuff about development of Poet A and Poet K is just to keep the critical industry going. It is certainly arguable that Reading gets better, he is more assured with his chosen instrument, but the noise he wants to make remains for the most part the same – "traditional values have gone to pot. The old hands have been bullied, badgered and baffled by new fangled phenomena... an arty-farty logo and the inevitable bandying about of cant and shibboleth by a bunch... at once callow and megalomaniacal". Good Heavens, it's New Labour, my local university, the Poetry Scene Now. Actually it's the feed mill where Reading used to work, whence he was sacked after twenty-two years service, for insubordinately refusing to wear the uniform. Now he's on the international poetry circuit and good luck to him. Reading is indeed Essential Reading. I suppose I only preach to the converted – if you like this sort of thing, then this is the sort of thing that you like. Is this a proper representation of Odysseus's justice? –

> He told Telemachus to fetch the slags
> and make them scrub the fancy furniture,
> clean all the shite and gore, then slay the cunts.

– Yes I think so. And mark the cunning of that literary "gore" poised so delicately between one of the "s" words ("a usage that's seldom got right", says Robert Conquest, but Reading gets it right) and the dreadful "c" word.

He started writing like Keats (not so very surprising because Keats was a kind of Elizabethan / Jacobean too), quite early abandoning Len Hutton as a boyhood hero, installing Robert Frost and then, unsurprisingly, Samuel Beckett. The demotic attracts him, that and the artificiality of metre and hard words (like "catafalque" you remember). He likes jokes too, jokes and japes (rather like Nabokov), translations of authors who are the names of fine wines. That was early Reading. And now, in *[untitled]*, he translates "from his English rendering of his own Armenian poem", the Armenian existentialist Vahe Oshagan, son of Hagop Oshagan, novelist, poet and critic. Armenian are they? Not Irish? Surely part Irish.

At the beginning of *[untitled]* there are seven runes. If they are Anglo-Saxon runes they say s,r,h,ea,w,d,a. Nothing for anyone there, as far as I can see. But they might be Danish or Swedish runes. Or I might have read them wrong. Or perhaps – as Reading translates Oshagan's English rendering of Armenian: "Is someone taking the piss?" Oh, I think so – don't you?

ROBERT CRAWFORD

Robert Crawford has consolidated his position as one of the most important writer-critics in Scotland today. Always hyper-alert to the Zeitgeist, his sole collection since New Generation, *Masculinity* (Cape, 1996), is a document in the growing reappraisal of the role of men in the world. In 1998, with Simon Armitage, he edited *The Penguin Book of Poetry from Britain and Ireland Since 1945*, and in 2000, with Mick Imlah he edited the *New Penguin Book of Scottish Poetry*. He has said: "As I've grown older, I've become more aware of a wish to write poems that are short, pithy, quite crammed, and of a desire for poems, sometimes long ones, that expand as richly as I can make them". Unusually for a poet of his intellectual savvy, he has no difficulty in writing celebratory poems, as in 'Scotch Broth' from *Masculinity* ("A soup so thick you could shake its hand / And stroll with it before dinner") or 'Fiat Lux' (below).

Mangan

FIAT LUX

Let there be braziers, holophotal lenses,
Polished golden flags, champagne and candles,

Let rays shine through the rose window of Chartres,
Let there be cowslips, myriad splats of rain,

Trilobites, new parliaments, red neon,
Let there be twin-stone rings and mirrorglass

Skyscrapers, glinting jumbos, Rannoch lochans
In which huge skies can touch down in the sun.

Let there be Muckle Flugga's phallic pharos,
Bug-eyed, winking tree-frogs; let there be

Grand Canyons, fireflies, tapers, tapirs, matches
Good and bad, simply to fan the flames.

Let there be lasers, Fabergé crystal eggs,
Hens' squelchy yokes, birch-bark's thin,

Diaphanous scratchiness, let there be you,
Me, son and daughter, let the Rhine

Flow through Cologne and Basle, let there be
Victoria Falls, Great Zimbabwe, hornet's wings,

Angels, cardboard, zinc, the electric brae.
Let there be both stromatolites and cows,

Llamas and zebras, dromedaries, cats,
Bens, buns and banns, let there be all,

End all, every generation, so the whole
Unknown universe be recreated

Through retinal cone and iris and religion.
As has been said before, let there be light.

JOHN MUIR VARIATIONS
for Les Murray

He hiked a thousand miles to a mountain daisy,
Then travelled, in a great tree, through a storm.

Joe's brush factory's flying metal files
Sliced out his eyesight. Light inched back

Gingerly, a thin, Calvinist boy,
Climbing the castle ruins at Dunbar,

Who'd emigrated from himself, one new
Disciple heading for a Newer World

Among Yosemite's iced, tip-top bird trills,
Riding avalanches with a tyke

Hitched to the universe. Last words:
"Sheep are hoofed locusts. Ban them". Now he's all

Pastures, moraines, pines, granite, and that odd
Small oil, *Madonna and Child of the Bullfinch*,

At SUNY, Binghamton, where the fat boy, tugging
A string incised on gold, tied to dark claws,

Rewinds yon unhurt bullfinch, flying blind
With zip-code neatness, back to Mary and Jesus

Who's never let go. It homes with a whistlebinkie's
Died-and-gone-to-heaven rush of song.

CAROL RUMENS

Carol Rumens has sought inspiration in many places: she began as a poet of suburban epiphanies, with a strong Larkinian sense enlivened with Martian touches, but she was drawn strongly towards Eastern Europe and Russia. In recent years, Ireland, where she has lived and taught, has been the dominant influence. She often invokes Larkin and his dilemmas of choice, with the difference that Rumens takes the other routes that Larkin refuses. In 'No Man's Land', from *Holding Pattern* (Blackstaff, 1998), a collection of new and previously published poems written in Ireland, she says: "Places are perfect to belong to: / They can't get up, they can't walk out on you". Her stance could be summed up as, "whatever I wrap my imagination around that's my home". She is aware of the vulnerability of this position – 'Spark City' ends: "[I] beg that nobody yet pulls out the wires, Demanding what right I have as a citizen / To claim the place where imagination fires".

STARLIGHT: A STORY

When we abolished nightfall from our cities
Stars by thousands died. Died like the small change
In the pocket-linings of a lottery-winner,
Or like the secrets of a world-language.

Never again would couples, naked-eyed,
Point to the true fidelities, dividing
Into the one who sees, the "nil" or "plus"
Dioptric millionaire, and the one who skims a wish-spoon

Through inner space, and smiles: "Oh yes, I see."
And yet our easy neighbour went on rising;
The massive dishes murmured: stars weren't apes or coral
(We blushed) but where we'd left the future niche-less,

North and far West, they peeped through the For-Sale boards
And swam naked in fields. Imagine it,
A land so dark the only animals,
The only birds, were stars! Back, we cried, back to starlight!

We made them ours, quick as the half-farmed acres.
We didn't ask, they burst out of the foaming
Tantalus of that clear black country sky
Into our lips, eyes, hair, mineral as raindrops:

Copper, quartz, sapphire, marquesite,
Brown diamonds, white. *Not in lone splendour*, no. We dipped

Into the bubbling universe of memory
To name the striding lovesick giant, the bears, the twins, the huntress.

Some of us found our god-folk, some, our folk-gods:
All the tutelary spirits of our sight
Reclaimed us, now we'd dumped the grid to mine
Our little clinkable purse of sixpenny physics.

But then we realised: darkness, too, was back.
At first a light sleep, a summer shower,
In weeks it gathered force and shapelessness,
Until the earth was plunged in endless nightfall.

We lengthened and diluted like our shadows.
We were the planet's after-life, its memory
Of dark-adapted eyes and hunting glamour
– Alerted, impotent. We snapped our press-stud torches

To spots of frost and listened, saw new species
Muscling between trees, and sighed for the sliproads,
While stars went on with being stars, pure brilliance
Of course but selfish, worse than genius.

Starlight. This, we've learned, was our illusion,
Oxymoronic, untranslatable
Into our puddled tracks and inked-out signposts. *Starlight*
That dies before it touches us, like love.

We swear: *de mortuis nil nisi bonum*
But each of us has stroked the reeds, confiding
To their long mouths that the dead have cheated us.
We pray, but I believe our prayers have changed

As prayers do change when a life-or-death desire
– That towering waterfall – no longer knocks us breathless,
No longer knocks at all, and we learn our little place
At the keyholes of ourselves. We are a solar people,

Clichéd through with the print of one near star.
These were our darlings all along: the rock-throwers,
Particle breeders, sperm-merchants, suns.
To every brightness, its reflective pattern,

And sight, perhaps, but not within our focus,
Our curvature. To us, the blank horizon,
The shadow where we look round for our neighbour.
When the earth tilts a little to the right

We say – or is it to the left? – we'll see her,
Luminous, unoffended, on our wave-length
Still, the only one we touched and did not haunt:
"The moon", we sigh, "what happened to old moonrise?"

RUTH PADEL

Relatively little known at the time of New Generation, with her two subsequent collections, *Fusewire* (Chatto, 1996) and *Rembrandt Would Have Loved You* (Chatto, 1998), Ruth Padel has become a force to be reckoned with. She won the National Poetry Competition in 1996 With 'Icicles Around a Tree in Dumfrieshire', a characteristically dazzling performance which spliced together Andy Goldsworthy's ice sculptures, the erotic, and the physics behind everything. Her latest collection, *Rembrandt Would Have Loved You* was shortlisted for the T. S. Eliot Prize and received a clutch of reviews to die for: "Her finely cadenced, beautiful fictions accord the hard truths of time, pain and motality their proper weight" (*TLS*).

THE LIGHT THAT MATTERS ON THE STAGE IS LIGHT THAT CASTS A SHADOW

So this was it. The dark star, death star, end
        Of world. And we were dinosaurs
On either side the six-mile-deep divide
        Where Himalayas bubbled up
In rose-red fission of the Earth's inside.

Now cut to physics. Squeeze that ball of gas
        We call the sun, compress
Its eight hundred, sixty-four thousand miles across
        Till all the atoms smash
And run,

And it's a white dwarf, weighing in
     At a tinkly thirty thousand miles diameter.
Squeeze again
     Till all the electrons melt and nothing's left
But neutrons. Now the sun you've got

Is nine miles wide, a neutron star. The only thing
     That can escape from it is light –
But light that's struggling, baby. Go on, do
     The shrink again, till the neutrons collapse too.
What's left is three miles wide. A skating rink.

You could walk it in forty minutes, easy.
     But escape velocity, the minimum speed
That'd lift you off its gravity, has passed
     The speed of light and nothing's getting out
Except black-body radiation, cabling back an S.O.S.

To our lost universe. Sable Véry pistols
     Shooting out from any object cruising space
That happens to fall in. If you dropped by, you'd be
     At once an elongated I, a ribbon of molten bees.
The closer in you got, the thinner you'd be squeezed.

There – that's the gravity of black holes.
     So nuclear,
So greedy-dark, you'd never have time to register
     The Gorgon-gaze as black.
That's it. That's where we were. An endless night

Of valedictory X-rays, not even a whiff
     Of God. Quantum cryptography, all chaos
And black light. But different for each of us.
     For you, the hell of neutral. Everything losing edge
And colour, a no man's mashed-potato-land of black.

No silhouette; no sexy *chiaroscuro*. Rays have to hit
     The retina for that, and you'd seen every light
Go out. As for me – I walked about
     Like a Polo filled with smoke. A zombie whose soul
Had been extracted and exhumed to tell of poisoning

By a *vaudoux* sorcerer, adept in the toxic bite
      Of puffer fish. Or a Spix Macaow, the only living thing
That spoke the language of a wiped-
      Out Indian tribe, who'd seen her mate,
The last recorded of her species, shot

For his cork-blue feathers. We followed separate
      Down-paths to the same dead spot, dead sun.
Where under some astro masterplan
      We then got back together, stumbling on
A switch we had to thump three times so halogen

Could well against the cliff. Look – rose-petal coronas,
      Scattering feathers on us of translucent gold
Like photons riding shotgun on a rainbow, warning us,
      "There is no meaning in your lives,
And no life in your hearts, without each other".

Even the wires of tension-calibrated steel
      Joined in
Saying, "Look, you two. You're very far
      From perfect. This is no solar idyll
You've got here. There's muddle – sin, if you like

To call it that – inside you both. Earth spins
      On its tilted axis:
The light you know each other by
      Will keep on changing. Yet the source is still
What they used to say God is.

Knowledge. Love. The rays that give this world
      Its ticking filaments and edge.
Light that matters on the stage
      Is light that casts a shadow.
Better now? That freeze-your-marrow night

All over? You both feel
      The winter's gone, you've got the dazzle
Back, full working order? Fine. But it's the Fall
      Sweethearts, the dark,
That'll keep you real".

Head and Heart

by Tim Radford

**A Quark for Mister Mark:
101 poems about science**

Ed. Maurice Riordan and Jon Turney

Faber, £6.99
ISBN 0571 20542 9

IN ONE OF the oldest surviving poems, God addresses the prophet Job from a whirlwind and asks him, rhetorically: "Hath the rain a father? or who hath begotten the drops of dew? Out of whose womb came the ice? and the hoary frost of heaven, who hath engendered it?" Besides being great poetry, these are great questions about the hydrological cycle. There has been, until recently, a lazy British presumption that poetry and science are somehow opposites: two separate bags, only one of which can be carried on board for the flight through life, the other consigned to the cargo hold. There is also a more distant implication that the words used in science are not the words of poetry. Not so: scientists tend to assume, along with Keats, that truth is beauty, and beauty truth. They use words like "elegant" and "beautiful" when they are particularly pleased with an outcome. Some of science's profoundest statements approach the pithiness sought by poets –

For every action
there is an equal and
opposite reaction

– sounds like a haiku in a hurry. But never mind the form, contemplate the content. Scientists, like poets, address questions about life, death, land, sea, space, time, love, and lust. Both may concern themselves with anything and everything in the universe. So anthologists who set about selecting poems about science have to decide what they mean by science, and which poems address, reflect, or respond to that science in some consistent way. Like John Heath Stubbs and Phillips Salman (*Poems of Science*, Penguin, 1984), the latest anthologists make a rule not to depart from English language poets, and then enjoyably break that rule. Each

anthology of course includes Miroslav Holub, the Czech immunologist; the Riordan-Turney selection also includes Primo Levi, the industrial chemist, who in 1984 was barely known outside Italy. The usual suspects (Donne, Sir John Davies, Christopher Smart, Samuel Butler) pop up in both books, and even the same poems, but rarely the same lines. So much for comparison: there are fresh reasons for buying Riordan and Turney. There is more science out there these days, and there are more popular and well-written books, conjuring with dazzling new ideas and more poets responding to both. For a poet, there are new images and themes to play with.

They serve revolving saucer eyes,
Dishes of stars; they wait upon
Huge lenses hung aloft to frame
The slow procession of the skies…

wrote Fleur Adcock in 'The Ex-Queen Among The Astronomers'; one imagines starting with the silhouette of Jodrell Bank in mind, but it's hardly a poem about radiotelescopy. Albert Goldbarth's 'Arguing Bartusiak' is about being married yet apart, and it plays with the imagery of spacetime as a fabric with holes in it:

sleepy at last, she
wraps herself in her blanket and,
if some of it, somewhere in it, isn't blanket
she wraps herself in that too.

Neil Rollinson toys with entropy ("your coffee grows cold on the kitchen table, / which means the universe is dying") but that, too is a poem about love. There was more direct confrontation when D. M. Black wrote 'Kew Gardens', addressing a dead scientist father, wanting

to say that the beauty of the autumn is a redundant
beauty,
that the sky had no need to be this particular shade
of blue,
nor the maple to die in flames of this particular
yellow…

in short, to say that the head can not always explain "these marvellous things that shock the heart". Actually, science doesn't do such a bad job of explaining either vision or the emotions, it just isn't very good at explaining the exquisiteness with which we experience them.

Some poems are responses to the world as supplied by science. Jo Shapcott's 'The Mad Cow Talks Back' is possible in that form because somebody first described a spongiform encephalopathy, and Peter Porter's Cold War poem 'Your Attention Please' is delivered, so to speak, by intercontinental ballistic missile capability, as first brought to you by Wernher von Braun. Old, almost discarded science delivers some wonderful surprises: in particular two seventeenth century women poets – Lucy Hutchinson and Margaret Cavendish.

The collection makes no great point about art or science, except that poets get more out of science than science gets out of poetry; and that there may be some pathways of science down which no iamb or dactyl has measured its tread, among them software engineering and plate tectonics. George Bradley's hymn 'About Planck Time' addresses that strange leap at the moment of creation, when the universe goes from no-time-at-all to time-already-begun. This step may be reversible, and if so:

it will all just
disappear, a parlour trick, a rabbit back in its hat
Will all go up in a flash of light, abracadabra
An idea that isn't being had any more.

How odd that a moment so tiny that it can only be measured with a decimal point and then forty-two noughts before you get to an integer, should produce an idea as big as that. But then the poet who wrote the book of Job was asking the same questions three thousand years ago: where did we come from, how did we get here, and where are we going, and why us?

Talking of which, I had half hoped for the biologist JBS Haldane's epic farewell to the world, the one that begins

I wish I had the voice of Homer
to sing of rectal carcinoma…

But perhaps there are some things that science and poetry do not want from each other.

SOME CONTRIBUTORS

Gillian Allnutt's latest collection is *Lintel* (Bloodaxe, 2001).

Peter Bland's *Selected Poems* were published by Carcanet in 1998.

Harry Clifton's prose book *On the Spine of Italy* is published by Pan.

Elaine Feinstein's biography of Ted Hughes will be published by Weidenfeld in the Autumn.

Lavinia Greenlaw's poem first appeared in *Last Words* (Picador).

Matt Holland is organiser of the Swindon Festival of Literature (May 1-12).

Michael Horovitz's latest publication is *Pop! – The Poetry Olympics Party Anthology* (New Departures).

Tim Kendall is the Editor of *Thumbscrew*.

David Kennedy is one of the editors of *The New Poetry* (Bloodaxe, 1992).

Peter Porter's *Collected Poems* were published by Oxford Poets in 1999.

Sheenagh Pugh's latest collection is *Stonelight* (Seren, 1999).

Justin Quinn is an Editor of *Metre*.

Tim Radford is Science Editor of the *Guardian*.

Ian Sansom reviews for the *Guardian* and *TLS*.

Ian Tromp reviews for *PN Review* and the *TLS*.

David Wheatley is an Editor of *Metre*.

John Whitworth's *From The Sonnet History of Modern Poetry* (with illustrations by Gerald Mangan) is published by Peterloo.

Graeme Wright is a member of the Bridgewater Hall writers' group in Manchester.

That Competitive Spirit

By Graeme Wright

The Forward Book Of Poetry 2001

Forward Publishing, £7.95
ISBN 0 571 20579 8

THERE EXISTS A popular misconception that a poetry competition anthology must consist of a few winners and a great many more losers. This not only sounds totally negative but, as this ninth annual from Forward Publishing, selected by John Walsh and his colleagues – Annalena McAfee of *The Guardian*, Brian Patten, previous winner Jo Shapcott and Bill Swainson of Bloomsbury Publishing, more than adequately shows, completely unfounded.

Yes, there are winners – that, after all is the *raison d'être* of any competition – as well as shortlisted entries in the three categories of Best Collection, Best First Collection and Best Individual Poem. But, more importantly, a large part of this book is dedicated to a section entitled Other Poems and it is here that the success of Forward's philosophy lies. In his short but instructive foreword John Walsh describes this as "letting the judges fill its pages with favourite poems whose authors didn't make the final cut". It is the ideal platform for new writers and those whose work demands a larger audience; on the strength of their poems in this book I look forward to discovering more from the pens of Stephen Dobyns, Helena Nelson and Dane Lavrnja as well as others too numerous to mention here.

In the opening section, the shortlist for the Best Collection, each of the five successful poets has two pieces and of these John Burnside's 'Desserts', Kathleen Jamie's 'Forget It' and Matthew Sweeney's 'Sweeney' amplify John Walsh's foreword promise of "something unexpected but equally rich on the next page". Burnside's poem crackles with the evocative reminiscences of childhood. It reads like a moist-eyed adult outside an old-fashioned sweet shop:

and something sharp

or incompletely sweetened
like the stalks
of rhubarb we would cut from old
allotments
dipped
in stolen sugar
reddled at the lips
and trying to imagine nights like this:
('Desserts', from *The Asylum Dance*)

For the shortlist which comprises the second section, Best First Collection, the judges have either been extremely fortunate or – and this is where the smart money is – they have launched five of our most audacious and original voices onto a much bigger stage.

Colette Bryce's collection *The Heel of Bernadette* had a mixed reception when it was published but the simplicity of her language combines so comfortably with her subject matter that her extraordinary vision tends to be overshadowed by this. In contrast, Brian Henry uses language the way Van Gogh used oil paint. 'Skin' from the collection 'Astronaut' layers words and images on top of one another to create a textural landscape of a poem that resonates with underlying suspense. Joanne Limburg's 'Out With The Muse', from *Femenismo* sparkles with raw humour and unrepentant honesty. In just twenty five lines she sums up the highs and lows of bohemia.

The five pieces in the Best Individual Poem section seem to be far more subjective, Robert Hamberger's 'Die Bravely' actually consisting of thirteen separate though related poems. In my view the diamond among the paste is Ruth Padel's 'Cascavel' a three-page mini epic that transports us deep into the mother lode of Brazil in pursuit

Of morganite from ruddy gobs of neo-slingshot.
How you tell a good one by comparing it to master
stones
Picked out by crystallographers. We want
Jewel-surgeons, droves of them, in action,
Making the perfect cut. 'Marquise', 'Brilliante',
'Classic Drop'.

The bulk of this book – as previously stated – is devoted to work which "didn't make the final cut" and it is here that the curious and the adventurous can discover some rare, new talent as well as hardy perennials such as Connie Bensley, Les Murray, Craig Raine and Vernon Scannell. Bearing in mind that inclusion in this anthology stems initially from submissions made by publishers and magazine editors it speaks volumes about the calibre of these that the likes of 'A La Recherche Du Temps Perdu' by Craig Raine and 'The War Graves' by Michael Longley play second fiddle. And what of Dennis O'Driscoll's paean to George Mackay Brown, 'Life Cycle' with its echoes of sea salt and cobbled lanes on every line?

July. Another wide-eyed sun. Its gold slick pours like oil

on the untroubled waves. Shoppers dab brows as
they gossip
George is drafting poems in a bottle-green shade.

It is tempting to compare this anthology with Forrest Gump's analogy of life and a box of chocolates but after much thought I prefer a comparison with a case of mixed wines; some bottles you know are at their peak now while others should be left to mature for many years. With this in mind the new millennium has opened with a bumper vintage.

KATHLEEN JAMIE

Kathleen Jamie's is one of the most confident voices in the Scottish poetic renaissance. She began as a precocious 19 year old with *Black Spiders* back in 1982. Perhaps her best known poem, the title poem of *The Queen of Sheba* (Bloodaxe, 1994), guys the traditional Scottish attitude (actually familiar everywhere north of the Trent) of distrusting anyone who "gets above themself": "Scotland, you have invoked her name / just once too often / in your Presbyterian living rooms". Jamie has always done her own thing, exploring Tibet and writing travel books about it in the 'eighties. Her third book, *Jizzen* (Picador, 1999) was shortlisted for the T. S. Eliot Prize. David Wheatley, in *Poetry Review,* praised its exuberant use of "post-McDiarmid 'lexomania'". Her use of Scots is totally natural, as in 'Bairnsang' from *Jizzen*: "We toshie man, gean tree and rowan / gif ye could staun / yer feat wad lichtsome tread..."

THE BUDDLEIA

When I pause to consider a god,
or creation unfolding
in front of my eyes –
is this my lot? Always
brought back to the same
grove of statues in ill
-fitting clothes: my suddenly
elderly parents, their broken-down
Hoover; or my quarrelling kids?

Come evening, it's almost too late
to walk in the garden, and try,
once again, to retire
the masculine God of my youth,
by seeking instead the divine
in the lupins, or foxgloves, or self
-seeded buddleia,
whose heavy horns flush as they
open to flower, and draw
these bumbling, well-meaning bees,
which remind me, again,
of my father, whom, Christ
I've forgotten to call.

THE VISIT

It's the small boy fishing
who draws my eye. He's been
kneeling on the dresser shelf,
with his rod and line and torn
straw hat, so long I've grown
to adulthood, had kids myself

but he never looks up. He's too intent
on his huge boyhood project
to heed the world, which is a back-room
with a hearth rug, a gas-fire, a mantelpiece
where three glassy dolphins
leap from a breaking wave,

where, though I'm saying "please don't..."
an old woman in a cardigan
is rising from a chair, one hand
knuckling her walking-stick, ready
for her journey to the kitchenette,
where she'll boil the kettle,

infuse the same dried-out tea-bag
she used at breakfast, then shakily
bring the hot cup; as I replace her fisherboy
and turn round, still saying
"please don't...", – but she's halfway
toward me now, and will not sit down.

GWYNETH LEWIS

Gwyneth Lewis is bilingual in Welsh and English and after being recognised as a poet in English whilst she was studying at Oxford in the early 'eighties published a Welsh collection, *Sonedau Redsa* (Gwasg Gomer, 1990) before her English debut *Parables and Faxes* (Bloodaxe) in 1995. Her second book, *Zero Gravity* (Bloodaxe, 1998) featured several poems about space flight. The mission to repair the Hubble is twinned in the poems with an elegy for Lewis's sister-in-law, and the conjunction leads to ideas from science such as the Doppler Effect informing an elegy. This year she was the fourth poet to receive a grant (£75,000) from NESTA. Her project involves a boat trip from Cardiff around the world, especially to places of Welsh interest such as Patagonia, the trip to be written up in prose and verse. Lewis has plenty to write about, an engaging and often provocative attitude, lots of chutzpah and formal gifts. Peter Porter has said: "Gwyneth Lewis amounts to a 'New Generation' just by herself".

Jeffrey Morgan

SPIT IT OUT!
(for Claire)

Their love couldn't save her, it was the knock
as they dropped the glass coffin. The shock

dislodged the apple in Snow White's throat,
made her start coughing. "Spit it out!"

encouraged Grumpy. Dock fussed, "Stand back,
I'm trained for this". As Snow White choked

on the poison she'd swallowed, facing death,
his Heimlich manoeuvre jolted her breath

and the purging started. First, a violent hack
sprayed out spittle, so the crowd stood back,

but a glob of the apple had shot out hard,
covered in mucous, lodged in Sleepy's beard,

where it dripped on his trousers. The company gasped
at the hosings of acid waterbrash,

then projectile vomit, a terrible black,
as her tiny frame tried to clear the block

in her oesophagus. Bashful caught her teeth
in a porcelain bowl he held underneath

her working gullet. Next came some words
in a private language that sounded weird

and then the objects for which they stood:
six saucepans, a tea set, then firewood,

a ball-cock, some money, a broken syringe,
twelve roughly hewn boulders from an unfinished henge

(they came out in hiccups), rusty nails,
two miles of barbed wire looped in bales,

then the artillery, booming out shells,
a Panzer division from her personal hell,

then a Red Cross unit. All round her fumes
from her inner corruption made everyone swoon –

rotten seagulls' eggs with a hint of skunk,
And then her waters or, rather, her gunk

broke, and she turned herself inside out
neatly, a clutch bag through her own throat,

her lungs a silk lining. Her tiny voice changed
to a contralto as her jaws' hinge

gaped and she found behind her lies
what she'd meant all along, not the alibis

she'd created with sweetness. The witch's curse
was shed now so, like an emptied purse,

she took herself back again with a gulp,
began to feel hungry. In a pool of gloop

the dwarves stood, dripping with day-glo snot.
"Did I say something wrong, boys? What is it? *What?*"

JAMIE McKENDRICK

McKendrick is a poet who likes to dwell on aesthetic decay (that is "pleasing decay", as John Piper used to call it). He has a longstanding interest in Italian poetry and the moods of Montale's poems pervade much of his work. His imagination is constantly making links with actual existing decay in his surroundings and the petrified artefacts of antiquity. In his latest book, *The Marble Fly* (Oxford Poets, 1997), his ancient car, having failed its MOT, is eulogized; "failure cum laude, rust-plaqued, cough-racked jade, / eyesore, ossiary, tin tub, dustbin". The manner in which his imagination can extract gorgeous imagery from the squalid everyday is sometimes extraordinary, as in 'Span', in which a trawl of the study's debris for a BT counterfoil yields: "...three golden dusters, bought last year / and still sealed in polythene, / their hems blanket-stitched with crimson thread / in a series of small 'v's overlapping / the dictionary. Crimson: it burns a fuse / the length of a dusty trail of roots / back to Arabic: qirmizi". *The Marble Fly* won the 1998 Forward Prize. He is presently working on an anthology of 20th-century Italian poetry for Faber. A selection of his first three books is published in *Sky Nails* (Faber, 2000).

SIGNIFYING NOTHING

It's a long way back from the country of signs
but I made it. And now I've almost forgotten
how to say *I'm old. I'm lost. I'm thirsty* . . .
though I keep seeing a figure who repeats instead
one gesture where the fingers shut like a fan

or the blunt fronds of a sea-anemone
– which means, at least I think it means,
spiriting away or downright piracy.
After that, it signals *nothing, nevermore, all gone*
by rocking the thumb like a dorsal fin.

Chances are I'll return some day, but by then
my hands will lie by my sides as dumb as lead
weights in a sash window or loaves of bread
and once again I'll be cast on
the patience of strangers, their opacity.

WILL

The ghost-faced, home-based, waist-coated
solicitor all but died of kidney disease
whilst waiting for our signatures

and then on recovery – a sign of recovery? –
forbearingly sent us a host of reminders
which we kept but ignored. So much for order . . .

we'd been adult enough at the outset
though his big dog with its anger problem
had threatened to leave nothing of us remaining

larger than a nostril or a knuckle.
The man himself looked to me like Gogol
or like one of his meek, disinherited clerks

whose existence is proof of the divine smirk,
but there was no-one to whom I'd have rather entrusted
what was left of my life, this paperwork.

So we willed whatever we should have thrown away
to each other in the event of some euphemism
befalling one of us. Which after three years

has yet to befall and the will, our will,
lies where it fell, always further under
the pile of papers on the occasional table,

a table not even occasionally a table
but a full-time pedestal for quires of trash.
All we had to do was pick up a pen

and, with the humblest flourish, write our names
but even that has proved beyond us,
would be an invitation to the unacceptable,

like an act of premature surrender,
like the signing of our own death warrants.

MARK FORD

Simon Martin

Mark Ford's poetry tends to elude easy summing up. What can be said is that he is fascinated by rock music, particularly Bob Dylan, and that, if postmodernism in poetry means anything it probably means Mark Ford. He has been pretty much the house poet of the *London Review of Books*. Ford's first book, *Landlocked* (Chatto, 1992), was in the tradition of Oxonian wit and hauteur but its gamey, exclamatory tone – "If only they knew what we were about to do!", "How strong they all were in those days!", "What a lovely evening!", "What a lovely life!" – also had echoes of Rosemary Tonks and the tradition of the insouciant flaneur: "Language *is* life (God help us). / It's more like vinegar eyebath to me". The over-production of cultural artefacts and the difficulties of negotiating them are at the heart of his poetry. His new book, *Soft Sift* (Faber) is reviewed on p.102.

"STOP KNOCKING..."
(After Charles d'Orléans)

Stop knocking for entrance to my thoughts
Care and worry, spare your knuckles,
For my brain is sleeping, and not to be woken –
Last night, you see, was spent in pain.

I must relax or I'll succumb, brain-fevered,
Please, please allow this poor mind rest.
Stop knocking for entrance to my thoughts
Care and worry; spare your knuckles.

As a cure Bon Espoir has devised
And had prepared a certain medicine:
I cannot lift my head from this pillow
Until I've had, at last, enough sleep sleep sleep . . . now
Stop knocking for entrance to my thoughts.

THEY DROVE

just terribly, but humorously sang
Jonathan Richman's 'Stop This Car' after each sudden

swerve or rubbery squeal. Once they discussed
the pros and cons of having sex

with Bob Dylan – or a Bob Dylan lookalike – in a Buick
while listening to 'From a Buick 6'.

Black fumes billowed from the exhaust, and by a species
of dead-reckoning they charted, in a road-atlas, detours

and punctures, losses and gains – it was almost
as once promised by, say, Van Morrison, as if to 'Hardnose

the Highway' were the same as to live.

Something Happened

by David Kennedy

MARK FORD

Soft Sift

Faber £7.99
ISBN 0 571 20781 2

MARK FORD'S EXCELLENT debut *Landlocked* (1992)
led some reviewers to call him an English Ashbery.
His new collection not only reveals that he is a very
different poet to Ashbery but suggests that he is in
many ways a more sophisticated one. Ashbery's
influence and tone are certainly audible. The open-
ing piece 'Looping the Loop' mocks any attempt
by the reader to discern an authentic "I" behind the
poetry or to decode easily consumable meaning:

Yet the affect hardly emerges, peers forth
Like a strayed mole through a cliff-crevice
On the unfamiliar scene...

Ford also alludes to popular culture and uses
cliché: 'Plan Nine', 'The Great Divide', 'Take
These Chains' and 'Twenty Twenty Vision' are
some of his titles. As with Ashbery, such titles are
chosen because they are, one might say, recognis-
able brands as opposed to accurate descriptions of
contents.

Ford's differences to Ashbery emerge clearly in
his opening lines. These are full of movement:
Ford's narrators and protagonists are seen flapping,

emerging, and riding. The speaker of 'Jack Rabbit'
asks himself in some agitation "Will I ever catch
up, or will I be easily / Caught first?" This is in
marked contrast to Ashbery's latest volume *Your
Name Here* where many poems begin in the passive
mode. Ashbery has written large quantities of verse
which seem both content with variations on themes
like "the affect hardly emerges" and unaware of
what must be termed the ideological implications
of detached linguistic contentment. The literal
movement in Ford's poems figures an impatience
with such repetition. The opening of 'Jack Rabbit'
also demonstrates that Ford generally writes
dramatic monologues, which begs the question
"what is being dramatised?"

Catching up or being caught are crucial in
addressing the composition of the individual life.
Ford's protagonists, like moles, are active day and
night in rapid cycles of work and rest but to what
end and in what context remain unclear. In
'Twenty Twenty Vision' the speaker "[realizes] my
doom is never to forget / My lost bearings". This
might identify Ford as a postmodernist but his
interests lie elsewhere. What Ford is dramatising
throughout *Soft Sift* is more akin to the old Dylan
refrain of "something is happening but you don't
know what it is". In 'Jack Rabbit' the speaker recalls
that "we were to police ourselves" but police heli-
copters hover ominously over the endings of other
poems. 'Reproduction' describes being out among
the shoppers but being caught "loitering with
uncertain / intent in the neutral, unblinking eye /
of a slyly angled closed-circuit security / camera".
The speaker's crime is to be economically inactive
and this implies the opposite: economic activity is
virtuous. *Soft Sift* powerfully conveys the way that
economics and business have become the domi-

nant models of human activity. The book is filled with terms like "tycoon", "corporate logo", "price sensitive data" and "the market".

So far, so subtle, but Ford does much more than just take soundings. In 'He Aims' "the sky lours / like a rival consortium" and "one is drawn to the far-flung, imperishable scenes featured / in a company calendar: veldt, ice-floes, desert // miles of prairie". In 'Jack Rabbit' "Prodigal / Sons and daughters stream forth in search / Of business". Ford puts economic language in the context of romantic contemplation, the sublime and the moral fable and thereby mirrors larger shifts. In England, business is now seen as a "blueprint" – a word Ford also uses – for everything from health provision to universities. Most importantly, business with its talk of "empowering" staff has taken over the humanistic vocabularies of citizenship and morals.

The book's location is unmistakably now and in England. 'Contingency Plans' talks of wrapping oneself up in "innate Englishness… like an old army coat" and 'I Wish' refers to the Queen Mother choking on a fishbone. *Soft Sift* also uses a recognisably English register of self-regulation ("we were to police ourselves") and "character". Ford's sensitivity in registering national identity and wider changes at the level of language is one measure of his originality as is his deft narration of the state yearning for lost solidity while being "underwritten / by an invisible host of dubious connections". This drives *Soft Sift*'s comedy which swings exuberantly between metaphysical wit, goofy aphorism and black farce. In this context, poetry – the formal enclosure of barely containable allusions – is uniquely placed to register our present state of imagining we can catch up without being caught.

MATTHEW SWEENEY

Sweeney has been an influential poet, writing strange narratives that owe more to Charles Simic than to the obvious local models to hand. The introduction to *Emergency Kit* (Faber, 1996), the anthology he edited with Jo Shapcott, serves as an *ars poetica*: "poems which discover the folklore and fable in our own time in the territory of urban myth, or, conversely, bring the light of ancient myth to bear on the problems of our own day. There are others which present wild, childlike tales whose distorting vision breaks through to the truth…". Sweeney is a poet of imaginative narratives whose poems often spring from someone else's first line, or a trapdoor of some kind being opened, then he is away on his fantasy. In 'The Volcano', from his latest book *A Smell of Fish* (Cape, 2000) he imagines a couple driving away from the impending disaster: "I put my hand on yours and squeezed, / thinking of lava / entering our house / and swarming over chairs / turning them into sculptures". True to his *Emergency Kit* manifesto he often promulgates cod folklore, as in 'Donkey Hoof' from *The Bridal Suite* (Cape, 1997): "Hollowed out a hoof will float – / give one to your favourite toddler. / The lightest donkeys walk on water".

THE BIRDS

That flat in Maida Vale
backed onto a garden
I walked in once at dawn
in a chemical dream,
hearing each bird singly,
like stereo multiplied,

in all the rooms of my brain –
so separate was each song
I sat on grass to take it in
and fat tears slid down.

And I was fifteen again,
insomniac, giving up at dawn,
pulling back curtains
to hundreds of gulls and crows
massed in the yard below,
hearing the squawks and caws
grow louder as the sun rose,
then, ten years later,
sweeten into this fanfare
no one alive should hear.

NEGATIONS

Style negates soul, you said to me.
I looked at your chic Armani coat,
your purple and blue Von Etzdorf scarf,
and wondered if I still spoke English.
Across the street a white dog barked
at a squawking, one-legged pigeon.
It would die before the day was out
whether or not the dog killed it –
and if the priests at school were right
it was a creature without soul.
It was also a creature without style,
certainly in its final plumage,
but didn't that mean it had a soul
in your mathematical scheme of things?
And weren't you shouting at me
that *you* were the one without soul,
or was this the blatantest of ironies?
And why were you using words like "soul",
you who espoused the religion of things?
And why "style", for that matter?
I just smiled and shook my head.
I reminded you about your train.
You kissed me on the cheek and left.
You didn't even glance at the pigeon.

RODDY LUMSDEN

Lumsden is one of the most promising poets to have emerged since New Generation. He arrived in London from Scotland around the time of the promotion and set about fulfilling the role of the post-New Gen poet (pace Don Paterson) with alacrity. He has published two collections – *Yeah Yeah Yeah* (Bloodaxe, 1997) and *The Book of Love* (Bloodaxe, 2000); a third, *Roddy Lumsden is Dead* (shades of Peter Reading), is due in the autumn. Lumsden has a nimble wit, formal elegance and great energy. He also has an appealing line in self-dramatization, as in 'August (And Nothing After)' from *Yeah Yeah Yeah*, which has Lumsden "overhearing" a couple on the bus talking about him: "I hear that Roddy Lumsden doesn't believe / in the soul...Is that no awfy?" Anyone with the chutzpah to do that is worth watching.

from 'CAVOLI RISCALDATI'

XIX   MAKING A GETAWAY

Surprising I should have – now sparks are flying –
The wedding dream at last, four years in coming.
Retreating from the banquet reverie
Where you sit posied on your bridegroom's knee,
Your mother greets me like a long lost son.
Then later, slipped of cream, sculpted in black,
You entertain my audience of one.
The limousine is waiting. Wish me luck:
I've spent so much in planning this escape.
One last embrace, then time for us to step
Across our thresholds. Yes, she's beautiful.
Yes, so are you. I only hope you've kept
The memories, receipts and, most of all,
Your promise of a file inside the cake.

XXII   ABACUS

...means "dust" – for once we counted on the ground.
And now I'm standing in the trees between
The banged-up icehouse at the Hermitage
And, moments on, the rock where Agassiz,
A Swiss geologist, came to displace

All former theories on glaciers.
This silence is immaculate. A log
Is carved into a bare-toothed, cartoon fox
For resting on. I'm sweating like a dog.
The unstrung beads of you seem all around:
Cooled vestiges of you. Look at my face,
Know you can count on me. At length, you'll learn –
Think of that glacier, biding its time.
Remember you are dust and shall return.

XXXII MAKING A SCENE

…which pans out from a pearl-glossed nail – Marie's –
As she slips back the sac of isinglass
On the Coolbox shelf beside the surplus ice
Below the rows of Bounty, Mars and Twix;
A fingernail, now notice, which reflects
A tall, swart-haired girl balanced on her toes
Upon the kerb outside, who holds her keys,
The space-rock fob of which imparts a pulse
Which gives her such occasioned counterpoise
And makes her thin hand shiver. My demands
Are this: that streams must run with dust and hills
Fall flat, that flame must thaw, that suns must freeze
Before I walk abroad in my own scenes,
Before I give an inch to my disease.

XLV HARM'S WAY

I think I saw her there, it's hard to tell.
You'd think by now I'd know the way she moves;
You'd think I'd understand how daylight gives,
How last-light thrills and fizzles, how nights fall
In much the way a face falls in a crowd
You'd felt yourself a part of, or a tent
Flaps cold and squandered after an event.
I knew I must not call her name aloud
(I knew I'd left a cigarette alight,
A conversation needing turned halfway
Through cooking, something I had meant to say
Before but hadn't felt the moment right).
I stayed, as in a lift jammed between floors
Where all stand stunned and waiting for applause.

FRED D'AGUIAR

Since his move to Florida, where he teaches at the University of Miami, D'Aguiar has been prolific, writing two long verse novels: *Bill of Rights* (Chatto, 1998) and *Bloodlines* (Chatto, 2000), three straight novels, *The Longest Memory* (Chatto, 1995), *Dear Future* (Chatto, 1997), *Feeding the Ghosts* (Chatto, 1998) and a play, *A Jamaican Airman Foresees his Death* (Methuen, 1995). His principal subject is the legacy of slavery; he often uses formal stanzas and exploits the humorous potential of formal verse as well as its grave and dignified one. 'El Dorado Update' from *Airy Hall* (Chatto, 1989) is one of the pithiest poems about the contemporary Caribbean states: "Riddle me, riddle me, riddle. / One people, one nation, one destiny? / Let's take a walk / not to stay, just to see...Lord, what to do in this fowl-coop / republic , risk my neck on a demo / or in a food queue?" *Bill of Rights* is a book-length poem about the 1978 mass suicide in Guyana by the followers of the Reverend Jim Jones.

AUTOBIOGRAPHY OF A STONE

I lay for a millennium in a bed of ice
until gravity dropped its sideways hammer
and opened a river in my bed.
The current wore me down –
pure one-way traffic.
I crouched and became set in my ways.

The river drained and dredged and dried.
Next thing I was broken into two by a complete
stranger who wanted my heart, its bright stone
for his lover. He discarded my two halves
on a mountain of such pieces
until a child's hand shaped me in it,

one piece of me in each hand,
then united into a right side pocket
in a warm dark next to his thigh.
Next in a clear jar someone took trouble
soaking the label off of, propped on a mantle above
a fireplace where I saw midnight love and its loss.

I could smell the lake and town reservoir
before he took me up, first my left side,
and leaned a little to his left and fired me
from the sling of his broad shoulder.

I skipped on the surface of that wrinkled lake
as if I fully intended to walk to the other side.

I wanted to reach the exact middle, that part
where water roots deepest and most still.
I heard him whoop and holler the number of skips.
I settled and waited for the rest of me.
He loaded me and fired again and counted
And exclaimed at the exact same number

As before: my walk on my toes,
the ballerina in me, me in my element,
my sign, my big bang in reverse, more air
than stone in those moments
on that dimpled face whose cold
rubbed me up the wrong way.

I fell together almost as neatly
as I had broken apart. All I needed now
was my stolen heart. I prayed for
that lover who owned it to find her way
to this lake, row out to its still centre,
drown over me.

Ready Salted

by Roddy Lumsden

Strong Words:
modern poets on modern poetry
ed. W N Herbert and Matthew Hollis

Bloodaxe Books, £10.95
ISBN 1 85224 515 8

LET ME EXPLAIN: this book of two halves is a collection of eighty or so short pieces about poetry; the first half were written between 1918 and the 1970s, the remainder are mainly new statements commissioned by the editors. The sources are diverse: some of the pieces are clarifications of poems or of writing processes, some are manifestos, some forewords, some squibs and spoofs, and some are reprinted from longer pieces of criticism. Of the forty or so pieces which constitute the first half of

Strong Words, well over half are by American poets, while most of the new pieces are by established British and Irish poets, most of whom are plucked from the middle-ground mainstream (a few more radical voices may have spiced up the recipe).

The effect of all this is like walking into a party where half the guests are old friends you meet (too) often and the other half tantalisingly unfamiliar, though which half is which depends on whether you are *au fait* with the zeitgeist or whether you are up on the century's poet-critics and curious to see what, in these pluralist days, mostly without movements, every man and woman has to say.

A book of this sort is overdue and anyone with a strong interest in poetry will want to read these pieces. That the commissioned part of *Strong Words* has a weakness may well be the fault of the book's budget. One suspects that, in some cases, a small fee was met with an equivalent amount of effort. Perhaps it's that, or just more of the lean-against-the-bookcase hauteur which too many of our current leading poets adopt with outward ease.

Having said that, to plough through forty straight-forward statements would make for dull reading. And it's not that the pieces which side-step the task of self-explanation aren't mostly entertaining in their own way – Michael Donaghy's wry anecdotes, Simon Armitage's fantasy of a bookless poetry, Sarah Maguire's poignant reworking of an Auden quote, Don Paterson's elegant aphorisms – but Andrew Motion's half-page vacillation and John Hartley Williams' lampoon manifesto are among a few disappointing inclusions. I'd have snipped them to make room for two delicious replacements: first, wouldn't it be good to have Ruth Padel "Ruth Padelling" Ruth Padel? Secondly, there's no one in British poetry who talks more sense about it than WN Herbert himself and so it's sad to see him here taking his editorial back-seat.

Incidentally, the first thing I looked for was Sean O'Brien's contribution. Surely the most able and opinionated poet-critic *de nos jours* would at least dip his toe into the didactic pool. Instead, we have an (admittedly fetching) assortment of squibs, poems and in-jokes. "That's not a manifesto, that's a sicknote", O'Brien says, spoofing the current trend for pluralist tight lips, but the problem is that it's so very hard to explain the what, why and how. Don't manifestos belong to squabs and libertines? And isn't talking a good game a sure sign that you'll fall flat when the whistle blows? Ignorance is indeed bliss at times – I try to keep my nose out of *Stillman's Poet's Manual*, for to risk knowing exactly what an "accent metre" is, is to invite it to rash all over my next six pieces. It's easy to convince one's self of a Monday lunchtime that the whole kit and caboodle of poetry is more than faintly ridiculous. I developed a theory reading this book that positions and beliefs follow far behind poems, that the business of poetics has less to do with aesthetic endeavour and more with covering one's back. The young poet who longs to pen a bookful of honed love lyrics, but finds what comes out are formless, dark narratives will soon enough be shoving out that third book accompanied by war cries of how the dark narrative is the only where-it's-at. Our voices choose us and it seems we must constantly apologise for their bad behaviour.

With all this in mind, it's not hard to find poets disagreeing in *Strong Words*. Here are a few to chew on: "The language of poetry is narcissism itself" (CK Williams). "...the lyrical impulse begins at the point of self-forgetting" (John Burnside). "What poetry mustn't do is talk to itself" (Bernard O'Donoghue). "A poem is a machine for remembering itself" (Don Paterson). It's interesting to read, back to back, David Constantine's plaint for the richness and otherness of poetic language and Hugo Williams' defence of truth, simplicity and a low style. That I agreed with both of them helps me none in learning the rules of this delirious game.

For stentorian voices, the first half of this book is more rewarding. They told it how it was in the olden days. Here's Ezra Pound, in 1918, leaping head first into the bathwater, talking of "principles", "presentation", "credo" and "ornament". Gee whizz! Here too you'll find a little of Frost's rumoured cold cunning, Hart Crane, still a heart-broke boy, defending his dynamic, Wallace Stevens' delightfully haughty aphorisms, Kavanagh's wicked sense of humour, MacDiarmid, the public lion, sounding off. Perhaps it's down to brash Americans and Celts, mainly male, of course, to stick the neck out in order to get it off one's chest.

The one non-statement in the book is a fascinating, short interview which Hollis conducted with Derek Walcott where it is suggested that manifestos and poetic positions are the product of the "metropolis". Walcott believes that it is only in big cities where poets feel the need to form factions and take a stand, eventually finding themselves able to write only on the wall they have their backs to. Is he right? Probably not, and anyhow, though faction-alism can be tedious, it allows purpose for some and, Lord knows, it would be dull if there weren't a few ready salted opinions.

This brings me to the two pieces (both by fellow Scots) which to me were the most engaging contributions. Kathleen Jamie's study of a poet's development surveys "the meta-process, the seeking of permission to move into new and difficult areas", producing a fascinating sally into the inexact science of those factors outside of the poem itself which bestow it with influence and confidence. Similarly, Douglas Dunn's top-notch essay, 'A Difficult Simple Art' comes head on at the whole business – how the self affects poetry and vice versa, how "the quality of the first-person singular" infiltrates the work. Dunn talks brilliantly too about how poetry differs from or replaces religion and when I found myself actually losing sleep over this debatable quote – "(Poetry can be) predisposed to recognise or discover but not to fabricate the mysterious...", – I realised that it probably holds that place in my life. *Strong Words*, with its two testaments and many prophets, is as good a bedside Bible as any.

IAN DUHIG

Ian Duhig is one of the few followers of Muldoon to have added something so distinctive it is possible to identify his parentage in poems by others such as John Goodby, for example, without any need to refer back to the example of the master himself. On the evidence of the two poems here, his work, famous for its "weird scholarship and boggy physicality" (Kevan Johnson), is becoming more lyrical and accessible. Duhig has been shortlisted for the Whitbread and T. S. Eliot prizes; more importantly he is the only poet to have won the National Poetry Competition outright twice. His latest book is *Nominies* (Bloodaxe, 1998).

FORTUNES
from the Anglo-Saxon

Again and again through Christ's grace
We borrow children from the night
And show them every face of love
And teach them the turning light.

Soon we're paying out their growth
In woollen clothes and shoes and caps
Too small a half an hour from bought:
What more's in store? For her perhaps?

See her a woman wiping her footprints
From the dewfall's silver memory;
She bears a child and injuries,
Wife to Jew, Gypsy, refugee.

He betrays his lord, is flayed
And crucified on the crossroads tree:
Hear him singing, his wits astray.
Your children burn out his family.

This one drowns. These grow rich.
She at twelve, all brave endeavour,

climbs high to reach a golden peach.
She must fall. She falls forever.

More than Cain's Clan bear a mark:
That laughing boy? Grief will break him.
The night is strong, our roads dark,
Christ the way. Take Him.

The National Poetry Competition 2000

The 2000 National Poetry Competition, sponsored by BT (First Prize £5000), was judged by Lavinia Greenlaw, Ian McMillan and Don Paterson with Germaine Greer in the Chair. Winners attended a prize-giving event at Tate Modern on 5 April, which also saw the launch of the 2001 Competition. Once again sponsored by BT, this year's competition will be judged by Jean 'Binta' Breeze, Ian Duhig and Michael Donaghy and chaired by Michèle Roberts. The closing date is 31 October, 2001. Entry forms can be obtained from 020 7420 9880 or www.poetrysoc.com.

First Prize

IAN DUHIG
THE LAMMAS HIRELING

After the fair, I'd still a light heart
and a heavy purse, he struck so cheap.
And cattle doted on him: in his time
mine only dropped heifers, fat as cream.
Yields doubled. I grew fond of company
that knew when to shut up. Then one night,

disturbed from dreams of my dear late wife,
I hunted down her torn voice to his pale form.
Stock-still in the light from the dark lantern,
stark-naked but for one bloody boot of fox-trap,
I knew him a warlock, a cow with leather horns.
To go into the hare gets you muckle sorrow,

the wisdom runs, muckle care. I levelled
and blew the small hour through his heart.
The moon came out. By its yellow witness
I saw him fur over like a stone mossing.
His lovely head thinned. His top lip gathered.
His eyes rose like bread. I carried him

in a sack that grew lighter at every step
and dropped him from a bridge. There was no
splash. Now my herd's elf-shot. I don't dream
but spend my nights casting ball from half-crowns
and my days here. Bless me Father I have sinned.
It has been an hour since my last confession.

Second Prize

CANDY NEUBERT
CHAMBER

The gun I keep in the underwear drawer
has a short grip; my little finger slips
right off the end of it. There are the four
chambers; it is like a heart, and it sits
well. It is for the white whale in my bed,
for taking him at night along the track
where rocks and pools long for him. Rounded lead
for the white marble mountain of his back.
The gun I keep in the underwear drawer
says Long John Silver – it might not be real
but it has a grey, unhappy colour
on the barrel and a sulphurous smell;
this helps him overcome the bashfulness
he feels about his size, and to undress.

Third Prize

ALEX BARR
LAND ADJOINING

Badly you want it I can see. *Duw* yes. Your eyes
are hungry for these great block gateposts and
my side of the shared hedgebank with its crisscross
mysteries of shade and unreachable spaces.

What can you offer? You will have to tempt me
with more than that. Forget what *I* paid for it.
Would a man sever part of a good handkerchief
lightly? Would he retreat from his frontier easily?

When I regard you sidelong with my hooded eyes
you do not see the fight in them. Small domains
have swallowed enough men with healthier bones than ours.
This six-metre strip could bury an infantry platoon.

Yes yes, that is a better offer. But still I hear
 your heart beat with desire for the hot pride of having
this long view from your barn conversion windows:
the sun rising over my lush coming grass.

Badly you want it. Good. Think of what you will conquer.
A sixteenth of an acre of pasture. A few timbers.
A useful sheet of iron. Two sycamores, an ash
in full, no longer shared. A rustling hawthorn thicket.

A family of reed buntings. A nest of wrens.
Beetles of many breeds. Ten thousand spiders. Access
to your barn's eastern eaves. A handy new opening
to your lane. (Isn't a wide gate a sight to die for?)

The air above will belong to you, not to mention also
that sharp upside-down pyramid of shale, magma,
nickel-iron and so on all the long way down.
No, I won't take less than the price of a whole acre.

IN APPRECIATION OF

Gregory Corso 1930 –2000

by Michael Horovitz

ONLY A FEW poets I know of were as self-taught as Corso, or retained such an unsullied child's eye (Dylan Thomas, Stevie Smith, Kenneth Patchen, Bernard Kops, Tom Pickard and Brian Patten are comparable). He discovered literature while serving three years for robbery in New York's Clinton Prison, and "came out 20 well read & in love with Chatterton, Marlowe & Shelley ... lived in Village & one night 1950 in a dark empty bar sitting with my prison poems I was graced with a deep-eyed apparition: Allen Ginsberg. Through him I first learned about contemporary poesy" (biographical note contributed to *The New American Poetry 1945-1960*, ed Donald Allen, Grove 1960).

Corso's early verse coloured my own beginnings with their risky juxtapositions – original images with antique inflections, surreal inventions with racy speech, fairy tale dreams with rough-hewn but instantly resonant word music – as in 'Poets Hitchhiking on the Highway':

> The apple-cart like a
>   broomstick angel
> snaps and splinters
>   old dutch shoes.

Developing his craft amid the ferment of experimentation in all the arts that animated the communal consciousness of youth in New York and Boston, L A and San Francisco, Paris and London throughout the 'fifties and 'sixties, Corso bypassed formal preconceptions to create his own modes of shaping sound: "When Bird Parker or Miles Davis blow a standard piece of music", he wrote at the front of his second book *Gasoline* (City Lights, 1958), "they break off into other own-self little unstandard sounds – well, that's my way with poetry – X Y & Z, call it automatic – I call it a standard flow (because at the offset words are standard) that is intentionally distracted diversed into my own sound. Many will say a poem written on that order is unpolished, etc – that's just what I want them to be – which is inevitably something NEW – like all good spontaneous jazz, newness is acceptable and expected – by hip people who listen".

Gasoline shows some of his provenance, as in 'Birthplace Revisited' ("I walk up the first flight; Dirty Ears / aims a knife at me . . ./ I pump him full of lost watches") and 'Italian Extravaganza' ("Mrs Lombardi's month-old son is dead. / I saw it in Rizzo's funeral parlour, / A small purplish wrinkled head. // They've just finished having high mass for it; / They're coming out now / . . wow, such a small coffin / And ten black Cadillacs to haul it in.")– and also his aspirations, with poems on Botticelli's 'Spring', Uccello, and 'For Miles':

> Your sound is faultless
>   pure & round
>   holy

> ...Your sound is your sound
>   true & from within
>   a confession
>   soulful & lovely.

And Corso's writing remained unashamedly romantic and religious, yet grounded in concrete and natural realities: "Spirit / is Life / It flows thru / the death of me / endlessly / like a river /unafraid / of becoming/ the sea".

When Jack Kerouac wrote that his buddy "sang Italian songs as sweet as Caruso and Sinatra" he put his finger on a finesse of articulation Corso did share with vocalists of their calibre (when Nat King Cole died, Sinatra commended his phrasing for hitting every syllable of every lyric "smack on the nose"). Both Corso's speaking voice and the inner voicings of his poetry were imbued with a virtuoso musician's precision – as witness his famous meditation on 'Marriage':

O God . . . the wedding! All her family and her friends
and only a handful of mine all scroungy and bearded
just waiting to get at the drinks and food –
And the priest! he looking at me as if I masturbated
asking me Do you take this woman for your lawful wedded wife?
And I trembling what to say say Pie Glue!
I kiss the bride all those corny men slapping me on the back
She's all yours boy! Ha-ha-ha!
And in their eyes you could see some obscene honeymoon going on –

     . . . streaming into cozy hotels
All going to do the same thing tonight
The indifferent clerk he knowing what was going to happen
The lobby zombies they knowing what
The whistling elevator man he knowing
The winking bellboy knowing
Everybody knowing! I'd be almost inclined not to do anything!
Stay up all night! Stare that hotel clerk in the eye!
Screaming: I deny honeymoon! I deny honeymoon!
Running rampant into those almost climactic suites
yelling Radio belly! Cat shovel!

Later the poem jump-cuts to other scenes, including sternly realistic ones he'd been – or would come to be
– all too familiar with:

Yet if I should get married and it's Connecticut and snow
and she gives birth to a child and I am sleepless, worn,
up for nights, head bowed against a quiet window, the past behind me,
finding myself in the most common of situations a trembling man
knowledged with responsibility not twig-smear …

    … hot smelly tight New York City
seven flights up, roaches and rats in the walls
a fat Reichian wife screeching over potatoes Get a job!
And five nose running brats in love with Batman
And the neighbours all toothless and dry haired
like those hag masses of the 18th century
all wanting to come in and watch TV
The landlord wants his rent
Grocery store Blue Cross Gas & Electric Knights of Columbus
Impossible to lie back and dream Telephone snow, ghost parking –
No! I should not get married I should never get married!
But …
…what if I'm 60 years old and not married,
all alone in a furnished room with pee stains on my underwear
and everybody else is married! All the universe married but me!

Like William Burroughs, Corso generally tried to keep his distance from the cock-crowing Beat Generation mythologising instigated by Kerouac and Ginsberg. Yet of all these men Corso is the one whose writings turn out to feel the least objectified from the booze-and-dope fuelled ups and downs of their author's oft retailed life stories. He repeatedly declared that "The poet and the poetry are inseparable". So where does that leave them after the poet's death? The persona fades from public memory, which Corso had begun to do since the 'seventies – as Iain Sinclair remarked, "a street poet in an age that has no use for poets or streets" ('Off-Beat', *London Review of Books*, 6 June 1996). But it seems to me that at least a dozen of his poems will be recalled and valued centuries hence – a precious few without which our living treasury would be much the poorer.

One of these has to be 'The Whole Mess . . . Almost', which he'd written just before coming to London for the launch of Poetry Olympics at Westminster Abbey twenty-one years ago: "I ran up ... to my small furnished room / and began throwing out / the things most important in life: / First went Truth", then God, then "Love cooing: / 'There's much more to me than you know' / I pushed her gushy ass out saying: / 'You always end up a bummer!' / Picked up Faith, Hope, Charity, / all three clinging together: / 'Without us you'll surely die' / 'With you I'm going nuts, goodbye' // Then Beauty... I told her: 'Move on'..." –

> Ran back . . and found the room empty
> except for Death
> hiding beneath the kitchen sink:
> "I'm not real!" It cried

> "I'm just a rumour spread by life..."
> Laughing I threw it out, sink and all...

The version of this poem in Corso's most complete collection, *Mindfield: New & Selected Poems* (Thunder's Mouth, NYC 1989, Paladin 1992) was considerably altered (not necessarily for the better) from the one he gave me for the first Poetry Olympics *New Departures* (Number 12, September 1980) – once again giving the lie to the common assumption that Beats never revised. 'The Whole Mess' resorts from the "rumour" of Death to "all that was left, Humor". Corso's egotistical sublime was indeed, unlike Wordsworth's more volu-minous one, mercifully often left in the shade by his delighted sense of the ridiculous. Thus he noted that "In the Mexican zoo / they have ordinary / American cows", and hi-jacked a direction sign-board from Regents Park Zoo as a found poem – reproducing as heading its arrow – pointed to: "Giant Panda / Lions / Humming Birds / Ladies". And in Berlin before the Wall, his benign observation antici-pated a rationale for world communion, one which the acknowledged legislators of our race could – and doubtless will – do a lot worse than file under Possible Saving Graces:

> The Berlin Zoo
> has two pay entrances.
> One for the West
> and one for the East.
> But after the tickets are bought
> they both join at the gate
> and stream toward the monkeys.

Alan Ross 1922 –2001

by Peter Bland

I FIRST SENT some poems to *London Magazine* in 1963, having emigrated to New Zealand in 1954 and published a couple of collections there. Alan Ross wrote back, curious about other New Zealand poets, and ended up publishing a small selection. A few years later he picked up on Allen Curnow's work, following that poet's brilliant emergence from almost a decade's silence. Back in the isolation of Wellington we eagerly looked forward to the arrival of the *London Magazine* each month, admiring its civility and urbane sense of style and enjoying, as contributors, being a part of that exciting "larger world" which it seemed to represent. The tone of the magazine – remembering that the 'sixties arrived late in New Zealand – seemed raffish, informed, and often liberatingly sexy. Qualities that stirred libidos repressed by the restrictions of a highly centralized Welfare State. In those early years Ross regularly published Auden, Larkin, Lowell, Durrell, Simpson, Porter, and Ewart (among other senior practitioners) and introduced us to newcomers such as Walcott, Harrison, and Brian Jones. As proto-colonials and ex-pats we were relieved to discover that the little Englandism of The Movement poets was clearly not to Ross's liking. His was an open and curious mind, always on the lookout for interesting minor talents as well as giving space to the big boys. One rubbed shoulders with writers as geographically apart as Douglas Livingston and Jaroslav Seifert, the latter providing Ross with a rare best seller when suddenly winning the Nobel Prize (London Magazine Editions' *An Umbrella from Piccadilly* being the only English

translation of Seifert's poems then available). His short story writers too, came from numerous countries – Graham Swift, William Boyd, Barbara Anderson, and Christopher Hope among them. Alan's own editorials and comment, usually on travel or art (Minton and Vaughan were among his early friends) were equally appreciated for their overt internationalism. Describing Hockney's work Ross writes "He is the poet of arrival and departure, of the impedimenta of the journey. Far from appropriating places he is the painter of vivid first impressions, a man on the hop. Some of the best travel writers have been the same, suggestive of movement not absorption. Three days were enough for D. H. Lawrence to produce his classic *Sea and Sardinia*, two weeks in Australia to get material for *Kangaroo,* a novel of outstanding insight. Real painting, like real writing, is done in the head". There's a breeziness and agility to Ross's prose, as there is to his poetry. The 1980s collection *Death Valley* being a good example of Ross the traveller at his dashing and insightful best.

In 1968 I returned to England after an absence of fourteen years. We met over lunch at one of the Italian restaurants that he frequented across the road from his office in Thurloe Place. He enjoyed treating his contributors to a good meal together with a relaxed mixture of booze, anecdote, and gossip. People warmed to his easy physicality. His shyness seemed, at times, to be almost a mask, something to half-hide behind. It offered him both protection and a point of view. For all his urbanity he had no side or affectation. One respected both his personal and his literary judgements. The magazine, which began as a passion, never – in spite of age and illness – lost its grip on him. It became, over forty years, so closely associated with the man that one came to regard both as permanent fixtures.

Alan's writing found its final expression in three volumes of memoirs published by Harvill Press. In these he mixes poetry and prose with fine tact, elegance and – particularly in *After Pusan* – a restrained elegiac quality that is often deeply moving. There's humour too in his work, often of an underlying surrealist flavour – an awareness, perhaps, of the disruptive role that desire, accident, and oblivion can play in everyday life.

In recent years Alan Ross lost many close friends, Roy Fuller, Gavin Ewart, and Stephen Spender in particular. Those of us now left with our memories of him have so much to be grateful for. Knowing he liked something you wrote always renewed one's spirit. Although an establishment figure he bore that responsibility lightly. One knew that, if possible, he wanted to even things up a little. Coming to England at the age of eight and, later, suffering some of the terrible inhumanities of war while serving in the navy, contributed to his understanding and sympathy for the outsider and the marginalized. The importance of *London Magazine* to our literature can hardly be in doubt. Its unique tone and broadly based appeal will be hard to replace. Already Alan's "home ground" in and around South Kensington and the Fulham Road, seems a bleaker and a lonelier place.

Adrian Henri 1932 –2000

by Phil Bowen

SHORTLY BEFORE THE first of his two strokes early in 1999, Adrian Henri came to Torrington in North Devon where I was living, to do a poetry reading. I met him on the Friday night and we went to the pub, talking, amongst other things about the biography that I had more or less completed about himself, Roger McGough and Brian Patten. There were several exciting gigs coming up, he told me, new publications, travel and a prestigious gallery in Cologne was showing his recent paintings. In short, a lot to look forward to for a sixty-seven year-old man, his customary enthusiasm for life, creativity – the sheer possibility of it all – completely undimmed.

I had been running a children's writing group in the town for over five years, and as they met on Saturday mornings, I asked Adrian whether he would mind popping in and listening to some of their work. My lasting memory of the man was of him doing just that without fuss or proclamation, commenting on the poems he had actually taken in, and talking about them in an informed, helpful way that the children both understood and took encouragement from. "Informed", "helpful" and "encouraging"– three good words in describing Adrian Henri.

The Mersey Poets were never a group, but for so many people that is exactly what they were. It was easier that way. You could have a favourite one like a Beatle or a Spice Girl. Imagine thinking like that about The Movement ("the one with the glasses") or The Group (the Who?). The Beat Generation Game!

But with the Liverpool three they were a bit, well, funny? Colourful? A bit dark too, perhaps? Popularity was never a problem. Being taken seriously was. Especially after the 'sixties. Not that it bothered Adrian very much. He was always working, doing what he wanted, usually at the centre of things. But he was shrewd too, forward-looking and observant. He may have thought laterally like a poet but his gaze was steady and cool, like a painter's.

Never one much for technique, in art or literature, it's hard at times to separate the poems from the life, but at their best they are blessed with the authority of experience – not simply knowing what something *is*, but what it is actually *about*. As a poet he was distinctive, and sometimes moving. He had his methods and they worked for him. The collection he will probably be remembered for most is his first, *Tonight at Noon*.

Perhaps somebody has already written a poem in his memory. Perhaps there are several. If not, there certainly will be. That's the effect he had. Even if you didn't know him, you thought you did.

During that brief visit to Torrington I suggested to Adrian a piece of artwork called 'Adrian's Wall', with all his friends contributing their own graffiti. Neeedless to say it never happened. But it should. Maybe the School of Performing Arts in Liverpool opposite his house in Mount Street should now commision poems to be written on the wall about a favourite son born across the water in Birkenhead.

One thing's for sure; few could do a better job than the man himself. So many of his best poems seem to be about talented people he knew in Liverpool who died before their time: Joyce Henri, Sam Walsh, John Lennon.

Fame suited Adrian. He was not only comfortable with it but used it to communicate some quite pressing artistic concerns. He *practised* inclusivity rather than paid lip service to it in the euphemistic arts / admin /management / political / comfort / speak currently and cringingly garbled in a way that makes you want to reach out for the nearest gun.

There is something warm and abiding in the itemising approach he often adopted. His poetry comes to life on the page in surprising twists and nuances that he did not always get credit for. There's something rather generous about those unashamedly sensuous responses.

My book was initially launched at the Chelsea Arts Club at the end of 1999. It was Adrian's first appearance in public since his stroke. He coped fine. Four months later he stood on stage at the Philharmonic Hall, concluding a massive benefit night in his honour, reading 'Love Is' like a hero. George Melly, Alan Bleasdale, Willy Russell and Carol Ann Duffy were there. Scaffold had reformed for the night – all so much different from the early readings Adrian had helped organize around the corner at Streate's, the beatnik centre of the north-west, back in 1961. Sinbad from *Brookside* was there, Brian Patten had reformed for the night, Adrian's iconic pink heart in the right place, at the centre of a huge, packed concert hall. This poetry Adrian? Where did it all go wrong?

Due to a recent accident I missed Adrian's funeral in Liverpool in January. I would liked to have been there. Adrian probably would have liked to have missed it. Maybe he did. Only time could possibly be the judge of that.

The previous January I talked about the book with Roger and Brian at Waterstone's in Piccadilly. As Adrian couldn't make it, Roger suggested I read one of his poems. I wanted to do 'New York City Blues' but there wasn't a copy handy, so I took the liberty of reading what I consider to be the best found poem in the language:

Mr Adrian Henri was punctual.
His talk was lively, imaginative and informative – enjoyed by both adults and children.
Unfortunately his personal appearance left much to be desired and did nothing to reinforce the standards of dress and hygiene held within the school.
It also did nothing to improve the image of Liverpool, a city in need of ambassadors.
(('Book the Writer')

calaveras calaveras calaveras
prance castanets click
quicken the rhythm of the dance
(from 'The Day of the Dead, Hope Street')

Liverpool Echo

by Matt Holland

PHIL BOWEN

A Gallery To Play To –
the story of the Mersey Poets

Stride, £9.95
ISBN 1 900152 63 0

ON THE EVIDENCE of this remarkable, dauntingly-detailed story of post-war poetry in Britain, centring on three famous Liverpool poets, you still cannot judge a book by its cover, much less by its binding and gummed up pages, many of which sandwiched great globules and slivers of dried glue, and came adrift when turned.

Now the book is read, it looks thoroughly beaten up, pages loose, back bent and broken. It is as well this was a complimentary copy, and a right good read, at least while interest could be sustained in the mountainous minutiae of Liverpool life and poets' relationships, and salacious snippets of sixties, seventies, and eighties social history, because *A Gallery to Play To*, that is the book itself, is not exactly a pleasure to handle or to hold: stiff, colourless, and cold, nothing like the glow of life that you get from the story it tells, nor the immediacy and warmth of the poems of Roger McGough, Brian Patten, and Adrian Henri.

Early in his introduction, author Phil Bowen sets out his stall, or at least that appears to be his aim, when he asserts that the challenge of this book is "to present a spirited and readable account of [the poets'] literary and social identity, rather than defensive protestations against dumbing down, or some belated critical exegesis".

Well, he does the spirited readable bit all right, in good and terrific measure, but can't help doing the other bits too. For example, his claim that the poets' publishing and performing successes during the last thirty years means "they must have been getting something right" and his choice quotation from Brian Patten, that "too many of the New Generation poets sound like tomorrow's academics" betray a need to articulate an obvious and deep defensiveness. This need is most notable, perhaps, in the very last line of the book, whose implication is clear as it concedes that the poets

"played to the gallery but at least had one to play to". And his commentary on poems, like this on the much-anthologised 'A Blade of Grass', which, Bowen says, "progresses with a strange truncated vividness, as if the poem itself is reminding Patten to obey subliminal instructions regarding his true ethical imagination", is critical exegesis in extremis! It makes you want to reassure him that defending something you like, value, and believe in needs no apology.

But boy does he go on about the poets' lives and those of all and sundry around them, in exhaustive and exhausting fashion. It is hardly surprising to discover, from a school friend tracked down by Bowen, that Adrian Henri was "a fat little kid with glasses, who had a strange sort of abstract other-worldliness about him, as if preoccupied with something far, far away". And do we really need to know that "another uncle [of Roger McGough's]... would encourage his wife – who had the onset of dementia – to tell stories about hearing Hitler talking to her on the radio" in order to better understand furniture-kissing 'Sad Aunt Madge'? You decide.

Nevertheless, as *PR* readers, we do enjoy knowing that, in the early eighties, arguments about gravity of subject and quality of achievement generated a hostility that showed that "the poetry scene was more riven by factionalism than twenty years earlier when the Mersey Poets had seemed such a problematic group", don't we? And also of interest to *PR* readers should be Bowen's reflections on the years he covers. For example, he reckons that the irony of the Thatcher years, "oppressive and philistine times", was that they were an opportunity for the arts to flourish, as poetry did.

But of greatest interest surely is the thorough, informative, and encyclopaedic knowledge, of the last thirty years of poetry and poets contained in this book. If the lives of poets represent a puzzle that you like, you will find that this book puts many pieces of the jigsaw in place.

However, if you prefer words in poems to stand alone and go unexplained by bucket loads of biographical bric-a-brac, then this one ain't for you. Also, it may all be delightfully anecdotal and too moist with the stuff of life to bear dry academic scrutiny of the kind generally favoured by dry academics, and possibly even New Generation poets, but it serves well, thank you very much, in giving a real sense of real people and their and our real and recent poetic roots. And it's also a good gossipy read. Yeah, yeah, yeah!